Ghosthunter

Ghosthunter

Adventures in the Afterlife

Tom Robertson
with Murray Scougall

BLACK & WHITE PUBLISHING

First published 2010
by Black & White Publishing Ltd
29 Ocean Drive, Edinburgh EH6 6JL

1 3 5 7 9 10 8 6 4 2   10 11 12 13
ISBN: 978 1 84502 313 3

A CIP catalogue record for this book is available from the British Library.

Typeset by Ellipsis Books Ltd, Glasgow
Printed and bound by MPG Books Ltd, Bodmin

Contents

Acknowledgements

I would like to dedicate this book to the memory of my mentor and friend, John McGregor. Job done, old pal.

It's also dedicated to Willie, Hughie and other friends who joined me or helped me on my adventures over the years, that I have either lost contact with or who have sadly passed away.

A big thanks to Black & White Publishing for this opportunity.

Finally, thanks to Adam Docherty, David Leslie and others who have assisted me over the years.

Tom Robertson

Thank you to Campbell, Alison, John, Janne and the rest of the team at Black & White for their help and guidance along the way.

A very special thanks to Neil Carmichael for all the time you gave up by reading each chapter as it came along and offering your opinion. You believed in the project from the beginning, and your suggestions and observations enhanced the book. I always looked forward to what you had to say – and you were usually right! I'd be happy to repay the favour one day.

Many thanks also to my fiancée Adriana, who spent her days off accompanying me around the many locations in the book gathering pictures, and in libraries and reference centres searching through dusty newspaper archives. I hope you enjoy reading the finished product.

To Iain Watson, thank you for the series of pictures you took of Tom, one of which adorns the front cover, on that cold spring morning.

Thanks also to my parents, who always encouraged me to write as a youngster. And to Bill Watson, for your encouragement all those years ago and, most importantly, for sorting out that comma splice problem!

Finally, thank you Tom for sharing your amazing stories with me. And yes, I know these are just the tip of the iceberg!

Murray Scougall

Introduction

'While much is too strange to be believed, nothing is too
strange to have happened.'

Thomas Hardy

What is a ghost?

Throughout my life, that is the one question I've been asked
more than any other.

A ghost can manifest itself in different ways to the human
eye but the simplest explanation I can give is to describe it as
an earthbound spirit.

All humans are built the same way and are made up of
similar parts but we remain individuals. Even our minds are
the same, they just contain different memories. What establishes
us as who we are, makes us different from our neighbours,
parents, siblings and friends, is the soul.

As far as I'm concerned, a body is just that, a unit of blood,
flesh and bones that only begins to function once a spirit, a
soul, has inhabited it.

That light at the end of the tunnel that the dying or those
who have a near-death experience speak of, I believe, involves
someone grabbing you by the feet and skelping your backside

until you start crying. That's because I think the brightly lit tunnel is the birth canal.

Every gene in a baby's tiny body might come from the people who made the child, but the soul? That's planted in the body.

I like to imagine the brain as a series of corridors all connecting with one another, but only accessible by opening the entrance to each new path. Most humans only use a tiny percentage of their brain during a lifetime, not just at any one moment. There's a wee door that opens for pain, another for fear, one for happiness, and so on.

Picture someone incredibly frightened. Let's say the person is falling from a great height and knows that when they hit the ground they will die instantly. The fear and overwhelming emotion searing through the mind as they plummet to their death must be incredible. Maybe it's all too much and the door that opens to the bright light becomes jammed, meaning the spirit doesn't pass onto the next body. Instead, it is stuck in purgatory and will remain earthbound, but unconnected to a body, until someone frees it . . . until the door is pulled open.

And that's where I come in.

In the next few pages, you will read about my first encounter with a ghost when I was a child in wartime Scotland. I believe the fright I experienced that summer's day in 1943 opened a special door in my brain and, from that moment on, I realised I was different from other children. In fact, I was different from everybody I knew.

It was as if I had an aerial attached to my head that attracted spirits.

As I became a man, I began investigating reports of strange phenomena, although it would be fair to say I was going into jobs like an angel that wore pit boots. It wasn't until I met a wonderful man called McGregor, who you will read lots about, that I understood the world in which I found myself and learned how to utilise my gifts. Not a day goes by, even all these years later, when I don't think of my late, great friend, the esteemed Johnny McGregor.

I don't know if any Tom, Dick or Harry could do what I do if they found that special door in their minds, or whether I truly have a gift.

What I do know is that my doorway was the entrance to an amazing life, where I saw things most people simply cannot comprehend; visions that would not be mustered in the darkest recesses of their minds nor in their blackest nightmares.

So read on for a collection of my most memorable cases, spanning seven decades in locations throughout Scotland, and remember, while these tales may sound unbelievable . . . they happened to me.

Tom Robertson

1

My Life with The Black Lady of Larkhall

'I have an appointment at this ruin with a man with a strange hobby. He exorcises ghosts. That's to say, he ends their existence. If existence is the right word to use about ghosts. If there are ghosts.'

Fyfe Robertson, *BBC Tonight* presenter, 1963.

I didn't know it at the time but my life changed forever one sunny, carefree afternoon when I was just seven years old. I was a typical boy, more interested in football than school; a cheery youngster full of adventure who could spend hours outside amusing myself. But something very atypical was about to happen to me on this summer's afternoon that would unlock a door to a world that would take me years to comprehend.

It was the school holidays, and I had just been invited by a group of older boys to go to the local orchards to pick apples and pears. I was excited, but by accepting their invitation my day – and my life – was about to take a sudden, amazing turn.

I grew up in a small Lanarkshire town called Larkhall, located less than twenty miles east of Glasgow. Looking back on its history, Larkhall was famous for the powerful Hamilton family dynasty, and then the development of the weaving trade in the area. Probably the most important factor in the town's development, however, was the discovery of the coal seams at the end of the eighteenth century. Larkhall became a mining town, with several different pits opening in the area. The mining industry became the lifeblood for Larkhall and employed several generations of families, including my own. I wasn't long into my teenage years when I began making a living down the pits, as did many other boys my age.

It was during the uncertain, war-dominated time of 1943; the day when I was asked to go up Morgan Glen, in the Millheugh area of Larkhall. I wasn't old enough to remember life before war began but I still knew that how we were living wasn't usual. Everyone knew somebody, whether it was family, friend or neighbour, who had gone off to fight. It was hard to think of anything else, as the symptoms of war were all around; the blackouts, air raids and rations. I can still remember the taste of Pom potato powder and the dried egg that was shipped over from America. It wasn't a bag I carried over my shoulder when I went to school, it was a gas mask, and inside the school every window had duct tape over its edges to reduce the risk of shrapnel, should they blow in owing to an explosion.

But on this day, the invitation from the older boys had provided some relief from the constant threat of the war. As I looked up the hill, my eyes locked on the once-grand surroundings of Broomhill House at the glen's summit. Built on the foundations of Old Machan Castle, which was destroyed some time after the Battle of Langside in 1568, the magnificent building used to be the base for the Broomhill Hamiltons. The stately home had been desolate for many years and was slowly falling into a state of disrepair. A fire, later in 1943, finalised its fate and left little but an incomplete shell lording over the glen, with the River Avon flowing along its base and the Larkhall Viaduct – at 175 feet, the highest viaduct in Scotland – casting a beautiful shadow over the setting.

Millheugh Bridge, Larkhall. Broomhill House, in its heyday, can be seen at the top left of the photograph. (Courtesy of the University of St Andrews Library).

My friends and I would play Cowboys and Indians around the glen. Sometimes we would play War, but not so often, as few would agree to act out the role of the Germans. We were prepared to go beyond playing war, despite our young age. It was mostly unspoken but I know my friends and I were willing to do whatever we could to help the cause. No surrender. We would look at Morgan Glen and imagine what would happen if the Germans came over the hills on foot; we would take them on and, in our young minds, thought we could have a few, as that was our territory and we knew every inch of it.

But in that moment, as the squad of eight or nine boys marched up the glen, all we were ready to do was fill our pockets and arms with as much fruit as we could carry. I was excited to be included, even though I knew it was only because I had happened to be there when they decided to go. As I struggled up the hill, trying to keep up with the longer legs of boys almost twice my age, I was instructed to be the lookout for any adults that approached. Even though the property was unoccupied, it remained private ground, so we didn't want to be caught stealing the fruit.

It might have been apples and pears that took me to Morgan Glen but, by the time I left the site of the old house, I had much more than ripe fruit to occupy my young mind. Because on that hilltop I didn't find apples and pears . . . I found a ghost.

This crumbling wall is all that remains of the once stately and imposing Broomhill House of Larkhall, the former home of the mysterious Black Lady.

I had climbed onto a part of an outer wall in front of Broomhill House that had crumbled over the years, and which gave a vast view of the surrounding landscape. In and around the decaying house, the huge trees, hundreds of years old, were overgrown. I could hear the voices and occasionally see the movement of the other boys through the branches of the trees as they picked fruit.

It's hard to imagine this partial wall, graffiti-strewn and surrounded by broken glass and sprouting trees, was once a famous stately home.

The sun was shining brightly and the heat penetrated the branches onto my head and neck. Adrenalin was pumping through my body. I feared someone might come along and catch us in the act and I would be in trouble, not only with this person but also with the lads for letting them down. No sooner had these thoughts passed through my head than I suddenly felt a presence near me. It was so strong and immediate that it made me jump, like an electric shock. I thought I had been sloppy and failed to notice someone approaching; the boys would never invite me again.

With trepidation, I shuffled my feet and slowly turned to look behind. I looked down to the ground from my vantage point and there it was; the source of what stared at me. I didn't know if the heat was making me see things or if the bright glare of the sun was impairing my vision, but it appeared to be a female figure, wearing a long, flowing dress, staring up at me. The strange thing was I could see straight through her, except for her face, and as I looked her up and down I noticed she appeared to be floating a foot off of the ground. Her body was just a faint outline.

It was, at that point, the most terrifying moment of my life. I was scared witless. My heart was thumping so hard I could feel my whole body moving and the hair on the back of my neck stood on end. The Germans didn't scare me but believe me, this woman did. I froze to the spot, wanting to scream but, like a bad dream, no sound would come out. People have asked me over the years if I was tempted to move closer, to investigate what she was and why I could see through her, to see how she was floating. Not a chance. All I wanted to do was run.

I don't remember many details of her face except for her dark skin and the piercing whites of her eyes as she looked at me. But then she smiled, and I'll never forget that smile. It was beautiful but it was also a knowing smile, as if to say, 'I know what you're up to. You're caught.'

I could no longer see or hear the rest of the lads and I had a feeling I was on my own. I jumped off the ledge and ran from whatever this was below me. I was so scared that I couldn't make my legs work; they were heavy and plodding. It was almost as if they didn't belong to me and I couldn't make them do what I wanted.

I turned round as I tried to drag myself away and she was still there, calmly watching me huff and puff my way down the glen. Its steep descent helped me gain momentum and eventually I picked up speed. I ran straight through a hedge, scratching my legs in several places, and again I looked round. She was gone.

The peak of Morgan Glen, the hill Tom rushed down after seeing The Black Lady for the first time.

I later learned that the older boys had spotted a figure through the trees and made a run for it, stuffing whatever fruit they could into their pockets, the rest abandoned to the ground. I didn't know if what they saw was the same thing I did, and since I wasn't overly friendly with the boys I didn't feel comfortable telling them what I had witnessed. To be honest,

I didn't know. I was only seven years old and the mind is an active but unreliable tool at that age. Had my eyes deceived me or the bright sunlight skewed my vision? I wasn't sure but, whatever it was, I kept it to myself.

I stayed away from the glen, and the house in particular, for a while after that; the image of the dark-skinned woman never far from my thoughts. But it was a popular place for kids to play and, over time, I edged my way back up the grassy hill. If I hadn't, I would have had no one to play with, as that was where we boys would inevitably end up if we weren't playing football.

It was 1946, three years after that encounter, when I met the woman again. By now I had learned that I wasn't alone when it came to having seen this female figure in and around Broomhill House and Morgan Glen. The story of 'The Black Lady', as she was known, was a famous tale in Larkhall and, by now, word of this mysterious woman was stretching farther afield as a popular and curious talking point.

To explain the origins of The Black Lady of Larkhall, one must go back further in history, to 1872. Henry Montgomery McNeil-Hamilton was born into the powerful Hamilton blood-line and, after his father died, became the last Laird of Raploch and Broomhill. Henry joined the military, served in the 3rd Battalion Cameronians and was a captain by the time he reached his mid-twenties. Around the turn of the twentieth century, Captain McNeil was sent to South Africa on service. While in the country, he encountered a woman, believed to be a few years older than him, who worked as a servant or a slave.

McNeil fell for the woman and, upon his return to Broomhill House, he had with him a new companion. She was passed off as a servant to the other staff and locals but it was thought she was more than that to the Captain. Local historians later believed they had found documents that suggested her name was Sita Phurdeen. Whether that is right or wrong, I don't know. I've never claimed to be a historian, but to me she will simply always be The Black Lady.

Very little was seen of her in Larkhall during her living days. She was never spotted beyond the glen, and the River Avon almost seemed to act as a moat she would not, or was not allowed to, cross. It was often said she became an embarrassment to McNeil, who had a rather grand social circle, as she was unable to adapt to the foreign culture.

Then she disappeared.

The Black Lady was seen late one evening around the house, as usual, but the next morning she was gone. She would never be seen again . . . at least not in the conventional sense.

It's believed that McNeil told those who inquired after her that she had grown homesick and returned overseas. But the number of reported sightings by locals of an apparition at the windows of the house or around the grounds soon made people question the Captain's story and wonder if she had left the estate alive.

In my adult years, I had the chance to speak to a woman who once worked in the house. Her name was Jean and I was friendly with her nephew, who told me I must speak to Jean about what she had seen at Broomhill.

Jean had worked on the estate as a maid after she left school. Her younger brother also worked there, in the Captain's stables.

The day after The Black Lady was last seen alive, Jean spotted McNeil with a basin full of liquid that looked like blood. Later, she saw him carrying a number of brown paper parcels.

Now, some people would immediately assume that McNeil

had killed her, dismembered her body and disposed of the parts at various locations around the estate. There were also a number of oversized sewerage drains around the house that led to the River Avon, which would have provided an easy way to dispose of her body.

Captain McNeil died when he was in his fifties, yet his passing was put down to old age. Was his premature death a result of a broken heart over the departure of his sweetheart, guilt over her death, or perhaps something more incredible, like a meeting from beyond the grave that frightened the very life out of him?

I was ten years old when I saw her the second time. I was playing in the fields of Morgan Glen with friends. I think it was Robin Hood, a typical children's chasing game similar to cops and robbers or Cowboys and Indians, with which we were keeping ourselves amused on that particular day.

I would need rescuing before the game was finished and a lady came to my salvation. But let's just say it wasn't Maid Marion.

The rest of the gang was chasing my friend and me, and as we thundered through the field I put my foot into what I thought was a pile of straw or dead grass.

To my horror I realised it was a wasps' nest. Suddenly, what felt like thousands of the insects were crawling all over me. I heard my pal yelling that he would run for help but I was unable to respond as I swatted and swiped. I ran round in circles trying in vain to free myself from the stinging embrace of the wasps. I fell to my knees in excruciating pain, my skin red and blotchy. Then everything seemed to go quiet.

I was on all fours, floundering like a fish out of water. My knees were sore and grass-stained. My head was tucked into my chest and the palms of my hands were pushed flat against the warm grass. I felt something being draped over my hunched shoulders and back and I thought my friends had returned. I lifted my head and looked up . . . and there she was; that same face that had stared at me three years earlier was standing before me again. She appeared identical to that first time.

I looked at my shoulders and saw a black cloak had been placed on me. I presumed she had done it. I lowered my head, exhausted, and closed my eyes for no longer than a few seconds.

When I opened them she was gone, as was the cloak over my back. Just then I heard my name being called and pounding feet running towards me. I looked round and saw my friends and the farmer from the nearby field. He had brown hessian sacks clutched in his hand that he kept his animal feed in, which he was going to use as a protective cover as he pulled me from the wasps.

'Who was that with you, Tom?' he asked, helping me to my feet. 'We could see somebody standing over you as we came across the field.'

I stood still as I tried to stop my head from spinning. My skin ached. They all saw her, too, I thought. I was relieved at that but I was also in shock and didn't know what to say about it all, so I simply replied, 'I don't know. I just don't know.'

As the years passed, I would leave school and begin working, start a family and generally walk the well-worn path of most working-class folk. But juxtaposed to this mundane normality, strange things were happening in my life; events I couldn't explain.

I was seeing apparitions. Ghosts.

At first I told myself it was my imagination but soon I realised that my life had changed when I encountered The Black Lady. It had opened my mind and I discovered I had a gift – in my presence, spirits would show themselves.

I began investigating hauntings in the Clyde Valley and Lanarkshire. The area has an astounding number of unexplained phenomena and local businesses or homeowners often called upon me to inspect their property for signs of ghosts. I was making a name for myself locally for conducting paranormal investigations.

I embraced my gift and began to fully understand it thanks to a remarkable man I met called McGregor. I had never heard of him until I went into the barbers in Larkhall for a haircut one afternoon. By this time, I had moved to nearby Motherwell, but I still came home for a haircut. It was 1959 and I had just appeared in the *Sunday Mail* for the first time thanks to a haunting I had investigated. My barber told me that Johnny McGregor had been in a few days earlier and had been talking about me and said he would like to meet me. I was intrigued so arrangements were made and we were introduced.

What an amazing person! He was a botanist by profession and ran a business selling rare plants from the big house he rented in Larkhall along with his mother. He had moved abroad for a time previously, where he designed a garden for a sheik amongst many other jobs, and he worked on Inchcolm, an island in the Firth of Forth, off the south coast of Fife. But his real passion was for the paranormal. He recognised I had something special and took me under his wing, helping me to fully embrace and exploit my gift.

McGregor was a highly educated man but he was also a little out of the ordinary. He was the double of Basil Rathbone, the South African-born British actor most famous for his portrayal of Sherlock Holmes; suave, elegant, slim and grey-haired, with an air of authority. He educated me about the world and taught me more than I had ever learned at school.

I was a dreamer as a boy. I had a switched-on brain but I refused to use it while I was at school. If I wasn't playing truant, I was staring out of the classroom window. When I moved onto high school I was barely ever in attendance; instead I worked on the milk cart to earn some money.

One day, when I did happen to attend lessons at Larkhall Academy, there was an intelligence test for all the pupils. I was in the dunces' class and didn't know about the test before I went in that day. I filled it in and thought nothing more of it and probably didn't go back to school again for weeks. In the meantime though, one of my teachers came to our house to see my mum. I had achieved the highest score out of all those who had taken the test. The teacher was amazed.

So when McGregor began to impart his knowledge to me in a subject I had genuine interest, I was like a pig in dirt. He was an immense, immeasurable help to me. He told me when he was younger he had studied under Harry Houdini and Houdini's long-time friend, Joseph F. Rinn. The latter was a wealthy merchant and an expert on psychical research who was the president of the Metropolitan Psychical Society in New York and the vice president of the American Society of Magicians. He believed all psychics and mediums were frauds and scientists and he would put on lavish shows and perform-ances to prove his point.

Houdini, in the few years before his death in 1926, also went on a crusade to debunk the psychics and would visit clairvoyants wearing a disguise in order to expose the supposed mediums. He infuriated Sir Arthur Conan Doyle, a former friend who believed in spiritualism and thought Houdini was a powerful spiritualist medium who was overpowering the mediums he was debunking. The two became public antagonists.

In Scotland, and occasionally in England, McGregor followed in their footsteps and exploited fake mediums. In time, I would join him on many of these cases. It takes a brave man to say there is nothing there when everyone else wants to believe it so much, but he did. He would book into seances and clairvoyants' sessions and expose them in the act. These con artists were exploiting the deads' loved ones but by the time McGregor was finished, the only person in the room who looked like a ghost was the white-faced fraudster who had been caught.

He was also a great hypnotist, as a group of drunken hard men in a Larkhall pub found to their embarrassment one evening. Despite his eccentricities and unusual pastimes, McGregor was a quiet man. We were having a drink with friends but this squad of boozers wouldn't leave him alone. They pestered my mentor about his hypnosis skills until he said he would put them under, if they wanted. The men readily agreed, as I don't think they believed he could make good on his claims, but he was good at what he did and successfully hypnotised them all. He told them every time he mentioned the Highlands, they would start dancing with gusto. Of course, when he brought them round they were of the opinion he had failed to do anything. Then he shouted, 'Hurrah for the Highlands,' and suddenly they were on their feet and on the tables, dancing. He kept them going all night, much to the delight of the rest of the bar patrons.

McGregor had carried out his own paranormal investigations but, after meeting me, I think he believed my talents and his knowledge could take us to a new level of investigative power. He took me under his wing and happily allowed me to deal with the public and the increasing interest from the media, since I was quite adept and comfortable dealing with publicity, while McGregor imparted his prowess from afar.

By early 1963, we had built up a strong casebook and my growing reputation had reached the BBC. The producers at the *Tonight* show – a nationwide topical news and current affairs programme that was the first of its kind in the country – approached me to ask if I would be willing to attempt the first exorcism on television. It was a huge, exciting proposal and I agreed to take part in this unique opportunity. *Tonight* was an innovative, live, forty-minute programme shown every weekday evening after the six o'clock news bulletin between 1957 and 1965, and was presented by Cliff Michelmore, who was famous for his closing statement at the end of each show: 'That's all for tonight, the next *Tonight* will be tomorrow night. Until then, goodnight!' It was watched by around seven million viewers throughout Britain . . . every evening.

What I didn't know at that time was the location and ghost the *Tonight* production team had chosen for the segment.

Of course, it was Broomhill House and The Black Lady.

Twenty years after I encountered the spectre as an un-assuming child – a moment that shaped my life and opened my mind – I was to return to the ruins of the once stately home and attempt to put the mysterious Black Lady to rest, with a sceptical national television audience watching my every move.

The day arrived and we made our way through the entrance to the estate and along the driveway until we reached the ruins. McGregor was with me and although he was briefly seen on camera, he stood back and simply observed.

It was a beautifully crisp winter's day and the sun shone through the tree branches to reflect small pockets of light onto the broken grey stone of the decaying house, parts of which remained standing, others reduced to scattered piles of debris.

The view from the pinnacle of Morgan Glen over the Millheugh area of Larkhall looked magnificent in the sunlight and reminded me of my childhood days spent playing in the glen with friends. So much time had passed and my life had changed in ways I could never have imagined since the first time I had stood on a ragged wall and looked across the landscape.

I visualised my younger self, standing in shorts and attempting to be brave while my heart threatened to burst from my chest.

I stood on the spot where it all began, my heart racing and my stomach fluttering as I waited to be called. This time I wanted The Black Lady to show herself. I believed I had the knowledge to exorcise her from the old house and allow her to pass over to the other side.

As the crew discussed angles and lighting, the sun suddenly disappeared and it turned icy cold. I looked up to the sky and felt flakes of snow land softly on my face. The flakes quickly fell harder and heavier and we all stood for a moment, open-mouthed, staring disbelievingly at each other, before attempting to take shelter under cover of the hanging tree branches. By the time the snowfall subsided, it was around a half foot deep on the ground.

Someone made the decision to clear most of the snow away from the area in which we were going to film, so we cut down some of the whin bushes that grew all over the glen and used them as makeshift brushes. It would have made quite the visual to have the snow all around us on this sunny day but perhaps it was cleared owing to the sensitive camera equipment. By this point, one would never have believed it had been snowing just minutes before as the sky was clear blue once again and the sun had returned. After the snow was brushed aside, we allowed ourselves a few moments to catch our breath and cool down, then the cameras were positioned.

But then there was another delay. Just before recording was due to begin one of the cameramen noticed the top of his machine had an icy glaze on it. He looked at the lens and that was frosted over, too. The cameras were frozen! The crew brought some towels and rubbed the ice from the cameras, checked they were working and, finally, on the third attempt, we were ready to roll.

With everything that had just happened I knew The Black Lady wasn't happy about the intrusion. Maybe if I had gone alone to attempt the exorcism she would have been all right about it, as I fully believed she was just a lost soul desperate to rest. But I don't think she appreciated the others being there or all the equipment they had brought, although she would have no idea what the cameras, lighting, microphone, or any-thing else that was on-site, were.

With the ragged ruins of the building behind me, I kneeled down on my right leg, clutching an open bible in my left hand, and focused hard on what I was about to do. Fyfe Robertson, the respected and well-known television personality, stood a short distance away and watched me closely.

'Earthbound spirit, what ails you?' I started, speaking in a clear but emotionless voice. 'Why are you so earthbound? Tell me why you can't get away. Do you hear me? Contact me. Tell me the reasons why you are earthbound.'

Now, I feel I should explain something at this point. I'm often asked how I perform an exorcism. It was one of the most popular questions I was asked when I used to give talks and seminars, and even people on the street to this day will ask me. I'm always careful about what I say because it isn't something that should be messed with. However, I'm willing to share a few details, perhaps as a deterrent if nothing else.

When there is a crowd watching or, in this instance, a television audience, then there is the pressure or expectation for a visual show. It can take on the demeanour of show business, because for a lot of people watching, that is all it is. They want to see a performance, but the reality is different. So when I said those words on bended knee and clutching a bible, well, that was for the audience's benefit. An exorcism is unspoken. It's a matter of locating the spirit, getting on the same wavelength and locking minds. I have to push myself into its mind or allow it to enter mine. Absolute concentration is paramount and distraction could prove costly.

It all comes down to overpowering it via the mind. It's dangerous and if it goes wrong then I could cause serious damage to myself. I always had to be aware when to step back, because if I could feel it becoming stronger or if I weakened then the spirit had the capability of inflicting hurt and pain. That's how they do it, not by clinking heavy chains behind their restless souls.

When I did an exorcism the heat that engulfed my body was horrendous; it was like my blood was boiling as it coursed through my veins. The energy I took from the spirit would flow through me in the form of electricity. I would tell clients, or whoever else was around, not to touch me after an exorcism because while the electric energy pours out of my body afterwards it takes time, so if someone touched me before it was gone, they were in bother. Some clients were so happy that they would grab my hand to shake it and boy, did they pay a price. On more than one occasion, a grown man was blown three feet away and landed on his backside after touching me in the aftermath of an exorcism.

I can feel when there is something at a location; a tingling, shivery sensation that courses through my body. McGregor would often experience the same feeling. As I stood atop Morgan Glen with a camera trained on me, I had that sense. I could feel The Black Lady's presence nearby, and while I couldn't see her, I knew she was there.

Fyfe, a tall, thin man wearing a long tweed jacket, a shirt and bow tie and a hunter's cap, approached me as I stopped speaking. I stood up as he asked me:

'Are you getting anywhere, Tom?'

'No, I'm not getting anywhere at the moment,' I admitted.

I was just twenty-six years old and appearing on live, national TV, attempting to do something that had never been done before the cameras. This was long before ghosthunting and the paranormal became almost permanent fixtures on television. Nowadays, it's almost impossible to flick through the satellite channels without coming across at least one supposed expert talking to the dead or stumbling through a haunted house. I was trying to do something that many of the people watching at home, and I suppose many of those in the crew, had absolutely no belief in. But I didn't allow myself to feel pressured.

I ran a hand over my slick black hair, a few strands flopping over my forehead, and went down on one knee again. I brought a tiny cross on a chain from my pocket and draped it over my extended right hand. The cameraman closed in on the cross and then moved slowly to my face.

'Lord, free this spirit from its earthbound ways.'

All of my concentration was focused on the task at hand.

There would be no more words as I trained my energy on The Black Lady. She was there and didn't put up a fight; she wanted to be gone from this lonely imprisonment. A moment or two passed then the atmosphere changed. I could no longer feel her.

Tom, with crucifix in hand, conducts The Black Lady exorcism in 1963.

'Amen,' I said quietly.

Fyfe slowly walked towards me again as I returned to my feet. I felt myself breathing out in relief, confident I had been successful.

'Has anything happened this time, Tom?' Fyfe asked.

'Yes, we've had more success this time. She's going . . . she's gone,' I told him.

'She's gone?' Fyfe sounded surprised, puzzled.

'She's gone. Yes, she's gone,' I reiterated. I was careful he didn't touch me. If there was energy running through me at that moment we really would have made a memorable TV moment.

Fyfe, looming over me, asked directly:

'How do you know that? And, more to the point, how do your clients know that? Have they just got to take your word for it?'

I saw the cameraman moving closer as I answered.

'No, well my fee is £2/10/0 [£2.50] an hour for exorcising a ghost and I don't get paid till six months have lapsed. If the ghost hasn't returned within six months, I will get my fee then. But, if it does return, I go back and do the job for nothing.'

At that point we wrapped up filming. I was thanked for my professionalism and for giving an insight into a subject about which little was known, and I made my way home, quite happy with how it had gone.

It was only later I heard the tragic news that had befallen one of the crew involved in the filming that day. The locations director had left Larkhall straight after we were finished, to drive up north for another job. He didn't get far on his journey, though, as his car went careering off the road into a fence and a wooden post crashed through the car windscreen upon impact and pummelled his chest. In what must have been a sickening sight, the wood pinned him to the seat of the car, killing him instantly. It was a macabre, brutal death.

Immediately, I feared The Black Lady wasn't gone after all. Had I failed in my attempt while the cameras were trained on me? Dark thoughts that she was connected to this awful tragedy played over and over in my mind. While she had never harmed me – in fact, she had saved me on occasion – I began to wonder whether she was more than a lost soul trapped in a world that never took to her.

Maybe she hadn't understood what I was trying to do, but

then again, perhaps there was a malevolent side to The Black Lady, an evil that until that point had never showed itself to me.

I would eventually be left in little doubt.

Time went on and I continued to juggle a normal family and working life while investigating paranormal cases. But The Black Lady wasn't finished with me yet.

I was enjoying a relaxing Saturday morning at home, looking forward to a day off work, when I heard a knock at the front door. I answered it to find two of my friends before me.

'Tom, could you give us a hand with a wee job we've got to do?' Jim asked.

'Aye, sure. But remember it's Saturday morning, boys. I don't want it to take up too much time,' I told Jim and Bobby, who I often drank with at our local, the Applebank Inn.

'No, no, that's fine, Tom. It shouldn't take too long,' Bobby said.

'So what can I help you with, lads?'

'We want to go up to The Black Lady's place and take the door lintel. You know how the Applebank is being refurbished? Well, they want to put the lintel into the pub as a showpiece.'

'Have you got permission?' I asked.

'Aye, Tom. Everything's all right.'

I took a deep breath. 'Okay, fair enough, let's do it.'

The Applebank Inn is an old pub that still operates to this day, located at the bottom of the steep, grassy hill from Broomhill House, overlooking the River Avon. Originally an alehouse when it opened in 1714, a retired seaman called Captain Morgan owned the establishment in the mid-eighteenth century. He purchased much of the land around the Inn from the Hamilton estate and gifted it to the people of Larkhall, hence the name 'Morgan' Glen.

As we travelled along the Broomhill estate's driveway in Jim's mini-van, I asked them why they needed me for this job. Surely some of the workmen refurbishing the Applebank could have carried out the task, or at least helped Jim and Bobby?

'They weren't too keen on coming up here, Tom, as they've heard the stories,' Bobby admitted. 'And to be honest, we would feel a little easier if you were here with us.'

I nodded my head, accepting the explanation. We arrived at the ruins and located the door lintel, which, despite the degradation of the site over the years, was still intact. It was a beautiful stone with swirling floral shapes around a square inlay, which looked as if it would have once been the location for a plaque. It might have been beautiful but it was also big and heavy. Very heavy. It measured approximately four feet in length, two feet wide and a half foot in depth. It must have weighed about half a tonne.

The boys had taken a couple of oak beams from the Applebank, that were to be used for the ceiling, and had placed them in the back of the van before coming to my house. We used the beams as a ramp up to the open van doors, pushing and dragging the lintel with all our might until it rested on the beams. We then picked up the two pieces of wood with the lintel on top and slid the whole lot into the van.

And that's where our troubles started.

The lintel was so heavy that the van struggled to move. The front wheels were damn near coming off the ground. So Bobby and I got out to alleviate some of the weight in the vehicle. I told them I would walk down through the glen and meet them back at the Applebank. The last I saw of the van as I made my way along the path was Bobby perching himself on the bonnet, attempting to shift some of the weight to the front of the vehicle. Rather you than me, I thought, as I walked away, wondering what I'd involved myself in this time.

I had only been standing on the steps to the Applebank a short time when the van slowly came into sight. Everybody and everything appeared to be in one piece, thankfully. Jim stopped the vehicle and we all walked round to the back and opened the doors and two of us climbed inside. A few of the workmen had come out of the inn and were there to assist us in carrying the lintel. We pushed and they pulled until it was out of the van and slowly being taken up the steps to the Applebank. Beads of sweat rolled down my back and it felt like my arms were about to pop out of their sockets. We feared the lintel wouldn't fit through the door but, with a little adjustment, we managed to guide it through and took it to the back of the lounge, where we gently and gratefully placed it down on the floor, happy it was over.

The bar owner was delighted with his new acquisition and our efforts in getting it to him and we, too, were quite proud of the efficiency with which we'd carried out the task. We accepted his offer of a drink but told him that while he was serving them up we would bring the oak beams back inside. Jim was to my left and Bobby to my right as we walked towards the door.

All of a sudden a shout came from over my shoulder, 'Look out, watch, look out!'

We barely had time to turn round to see what we were being warned of before it happened.

Jim jumped to his left and Bobby scampered to his right. The only way I could go was out the front door and down the steep steps to the road. But there was no time. I was struck down, knocked through the door and left in a heap.

It was a few moments before I regained consciousness. When I woke I found myself at the bottom of the steps. I ached all over and struggled to sit upright and knew I was in a bad state.

There was only one way I was leaving this spot and that was in an ambulance.

When I raised my head gingerly from the uncomfortable bed in Stonehouse Hospital a short while later, I struggled to deal with the story I had been told on the way to the hospital. I looked at the drip in my arm and wondered if the cocktail of painkillers the doctors had administered was making my mind hazy. As I slowly came round, the story became clearer in my head and haunted my drug-induced dreams.

The hulking lintel that Jim, Bobby and I had placed on the pub floor had risen off the ground as we walked away and had flown through the air towards the front of the pub. It struck me in the back and sent me hurtling about ten feet. The lintel crashed to the ground afterwards but remained intact.

My spine was damaged from the blow and it took me a long while to recuperate. As I lay in that hospital bed I convinced myself The Black Lady was behind the lintel attack and had purposefully attacked me. I decided the moment I was fit and able I would return to the Applebank. It was like falling off a horse; if I didn't get back in the saddle as soon as possible then the fear and trepidation would build and that could spell the end.

Sometime later, I visited the Applebank Inn, clutching the walking sticks I still required, and saw the lintel had been cemented into an alcove in a corner of the lounge. I had my picture taken beside it as a reminder of the incident, not that I needed one, and it ended up appearing in the press. My injury was a warning I intended to heed. I would be removing nothing else from the site of Broomhill House, and I never have.

★

The media interest in The Black Lady and specifically my long connection to it remained. I was occasionally asked to assist with a newspaper article or was interviewed for television about the Lady but, in general, I decided to give her a wide berth. She had proved on two occasions just how dangerous and vengeful she could be when angered. And there was, of course, the mystery of Captain McNeil's premature death.

My vow to stay away faltered while I was out having a relaxing walk one day in the summer of 1990. I had just received a new camera in the post after sending off the coupons that used to come inside cigarette packets, which basically encouraged people to smoke more in order to obtain a free gift. It didn't look especially good; it was bright red and plastic, not particularly sturdy, but I thought I would try it out since looks can be deceptive.

I was strolling through Larkhall, down by the River Avon, when I encountered two friends I hadn't seen for a long time. They had been fishing and said they were going to take a walk up Morgan Glen to The Black Lady's place to sit and admire the sprawling views on this blue-sky day before going home to cook their catches. They asked me to join them and, perhaps a little reticently, I agreed. We made our way to Broomhill House and sat down on some of the loose stones from the house. Only a few small sections of the building remained standing amongst the overgrowth and these stones had been sprayed with graffiti.

We had been sitting for around ten minutes, chatting and gazing over the landscape and reminiscing about our younger days, when it happened.

I spotted something moving behind the overhanging tree branches. I knew it wasn't the wind because there wasn't even a breeze. I looked at the two men beside me and could tell by the concerned looks on their faces that they saw it, too. I stood up and brought the camera from my pocket. I knew who this was, even though I didn't have a clear view yet.

'That's her, boys,' I said in a whisper, moving slowly and quietly towards The Black Lady as her weak image came into sight.

She was walking away from us, on the other side of some trees. I followed her and the two men followed me, visibly upset at what was happening but sticking beside me in a perhaps misjudged view that they would be better off by my side.

We moved towards the trees and there she was, visible through the branches, just as I remembered her. I had my camera gripped between my hands, its hard plastic corners digging into my palms. I moved a little closer but my two friends didn't budge. I lifted the camera to eye level and pressed down the button. Snap. I rolled the spool on and took another shot. Then she was gone, vanished.

I couldn't believe I had taken a picture of The Black Lady. It was almost as if she had allowed me. I didn't know what she was doing, and in that moment I didn't care, I was just desperate to see the pictures. I ushered my shocked friends, whose stunned silence was only disturbed by the occasional swear word, down the glen. I left them as soon as we reached the bottom, their appetites for the fish in their boxes long gone, and made my way to the nearest photo lab. The spool wasn't close to being finished but I didn't care, I had to see these photos.

When they were developed I gripped the six-by-fours and stared at the images for a long time. There she was, through the branches but visible all the same, the ghostly image of The Black Lady. I had a few friends in the press and I contacted

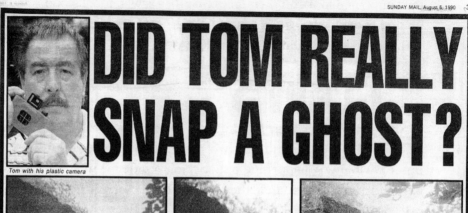

SUNDAY MAIL, August 5, 1990 3

DID TOM REALLY SNAP A GHOST?

Tom with his plastic camera

GHOSTLY *The eerie figure of the restless Black Lady appears at the ruins*

GHASTLY *The sinister shape seems to turn away*

GONE *A picture of the haunting spot taken by a Sunday Mail photographer*

By MARION SCOTT

GHOSTBUSTER Tom Robertson claims he has caught the spook which has haunted him almost all his life.

He took these scary snaps with a tiny plastic camera bought with cigarette coupons.

And he claims they show the spine-chilling form of the Black Lady of Larkhall.

They were taken last Thursday night at the creepy ruins of Broomhill House in Larkhall, Lanarkshire.

The frightening spectacle was also witnessed by two men returning from a fishing trip.

Sunday Mail Deputy Picture Editor David Robertson has spent hours examining the photographs and negatives.

And he said: "Photographically these have not been tampered with in any way.

"It would have been impossible for these size of negatives to be tampered with and particularly by the men who took them who

Mystery of spooky Black Lady

have no expertise in the field."

But Tom has bad memories of tangling with the restless Black Lady before ... he says she left him crippled.

Tom had helped remove a stone coat of arms from the ruin 15 years ago. He said: "We got it into a nearby pub.

GRAVE

"As we walked away, the stone flew through the air of it's own accord and smashed my spine, leaving me crippled."

Tom – who has spent a lifetime chasing ghosts and evil spirits all over the country – said: "I'll defy anyone to say it's not genuine.

"The ghost was at the ruined window where the Black Lady was often seen. She's a very sinister spirit."

One of the witnesses Hugh O'Donnell, 53, of West Clyde Street, Larkhall, said: "It floated around for about 15 minutes.

"We got scared but took the pictures with the camera we use to snap our fishing catches."

Yesterday we took Tom, 55, of Burnhead Road, Larkhall, back to the site with Daphne and John Plowman – experts from the Scottish Society for Psychical Research.

And they're convinced it was a visitor from beyond the grave.

Daphne said: "It's very rare to get pictures like these and a hoax would require a great deal of elaborate planning."

Jeanie Gilmour, 71, of Dalkieth was a housemaid at Broomhill House. She says the Black Lady was a girl brought from Ceylon in the 1920's by a wealthy seaman.

She added: "We heard Captain McNeill had got her pregnant. She disappeared and we believed she'd been murdered.

"I was 15 when I first saw her ghost. It came up to my room and disappeared through a wall."

Photographic evidence of the Black Lady as it appeared in the Sunday Mail *in August 1990.*

28

one who worked with the *Sunday Mail* to let him have a look at the pictures. Everyone I showed the photos to was excited and he was no different. He gave them to his pictures editor, who confirmed they hadn't been tampered with, and that weekend they were printed in the newspaper.

The feedback and interest was tremendous. I was contacted by BBC Scotland, who asked me to appear on their lunchtime *Garden Party* show, which was filmed live in Glasgow's Botanic Gardens, across the road from the station's old headquarters on Queen Margaret Drive. I put on my best suit and placed the red plastic camera in my pocket.

I arrived at the BBC studios where I was told the details and format for the show. By coincidence, the director of that day's programme was a gentleman called David Martin, the same reporter who had done that first story with me, for the *Sunday Mail* in the late 1950s, that had caught the eye of McGregor. In a further case of serendipity, this was to be David's last job before retiring and it put me at ease to know he was the man behind the camera. I was taken to the Green Room and found I was the first person to arrive. Bob Geldof was the other featured guest on the episode and he arrived in the room soon afterwards. He was to be interviewed by former Skids man Richard Jobson, now a renowned film director, and would perform a song with his band on the old railway platform under the Botanics.

Geldof and I didn't say much as we passed each other in the green room.

I was led on to the makeshift set in the Gardens and sat down in the chair where I would be interviewed; we went live a few minutes later and I told the interviewer how I had come to take the photos.

He asked me to show the viewers the camera and I brought

it from my pocket and explained I had purchased it using cigarette coupons. I reassured him the photos had not been tampered with after he stated that sceptics would have big doubts over the validity of the pictures. Then he asked me, bearing in mind the number of doubters, why I had been doing this for so many years and if it was a compulsion?

'Well, I don't know,' I admitted.

It's something that goes back to when I was seven years of age. I was a normal boy but strange things seemed to happen to me. When I'm about, things happen. It's not like reading a book . . . you're taught to read books. I believe this is something you are born with and can't pass on to anyone else.

Over the years, I was often asked about The Black Lady. Our names had become synonymous with each other across several decades, for better or worse. For all the cases I've investigated and strange events I've found myself part of, The Black Lady of Broomhill House always crops up in conversations about my work.

As I grew older I no longer carried out as many investigations as I did in my younger days. I made the decision that if someone came to me, desperate for help, then I would endeavour to do what I could for that individual, but I wouldn't go looking for cases. Unfortunately, I have never come across a successor, someone who has that gift, like McGregor had found in me.

Several years ago, an old friend asked me if I would like to collaborate on an amateur documentary about my life. He had all of the recording equipment and was keen, so I agreed and we had a few conversations about what the film should contain. Obviously The Black Lady came up early in our talks. He told me he had never been to Broomhill House and would like to visit the area to gain a feel for the place. He intended going up the glen with his camera to take some shots of the famous site and asked me to accompany him, in order to show him where I had seen her over the years.

I refused and advised against visiting Broomhill House. I knew exactly what she was capable of by now and I was at a stage in my life when I didn't fancy crossing her again. My friend was adamant about it, though. I don't think he quite believed what I was warning him against and, against my wishes, he made the decision to go alone.

A short time after his visit to Broomhill House, he collapsed at home and suffered a massive brain haemorrhage. I was shocked and horrified when I heard, and not just because my friend was seriously ill. I immediately thought of The Black Lady and the BBC locations director decades earlier, and asked myself if this tragedy that had befallen my friend was simply a sad coincidence.

I couldn't be sure about it but, thankfully, after a long battle, my friend survived the illness.

A few years later, in the summer of 2007, I was introduced to a singer called Joann Gilmartin. Originally from Lanark, this fabulous singer moved to the States and found success as one of the most in-demand performers at Burns Suppers throughout California and the West Coast. As well as that, she is a children's author and has her own Scottish-themed show on a national television channel called PBS.

Joann was back in Scotland to visit her mum, to conduct a sightseeing tour for American visitors and to film a special episode of her television show, when we were introduced through a mutual friend. After talking for a while and hearing about my career, she decided I should be the subject of one of the show's segments. We met in the old Cathedral House Hotel, across from the famous Necropolis cemetery in Glasgow, to film the interview. As we chatted off camera, she asked about The Black Lady and, perhaps foolishly, I told her all about our history, but I warned Joann I didn't feel it was safe to do a TV show about the spirit.

'Don't worry, Tom, I'm not frightened,' Joann told me, perhaps thinking I was just an old superstitious man.

We finished the recorded interview, had a chat and a cup of tea, and parted ways. A few days later she returned to Los Angeles, looking forward to editing the material with her production team and broadcasting it to her huge audience.

But Joann didn't get so far as the studio. Call it fate, call it bad luck, I call it The Black Lady.

She was driving through Los Angeles when a vehicle blind-sided her and smashed into her car, leaving it no more than a mangled and twisted piece of metal, with Joann stuck inside. The emergency services freed her from the wreckage and rushed her to hospital, where she spent several days in intensive care. She would survive but the injuries she suffered that day will take a long time to heal, if ever, and she has been unable to return to her television work. The episode we filmed remains in storage and might never be shown. The news from across the Atlantic struck a nerve with me and, perhaps feeling a little responsible, I asked myself, how long could I let this carry on?

It had been a long time since I walked along the old driveway or climbed Morgan Glen to stand in the ruins of Broomhill House. I was seventy-one years old, not as fit or as fast as I used to be.

I live in a small, isolated cottage in rural Lanarkshire, several miles from Larkhall and Broomhill House. Several miles from anywhere, truth be told, but that's the way I like it. However, on a cold, wet Friday evening, The Black Lady was as close to me as she had ever been, at least in my thoughts. The rain that lashed against my roof and onto the empty road that I could see from my chair provided a background noise to the thoughts playing over and over in my mind. Now, I felt, was the moment to go back. The point had been reached where I had to go back. It was time to finish this, once and for all.

I pulled on my boots and waterproof coat, grabbed my car keys and mobile phone from the table, and took a deep breath. I informed my daughter, who lives with me, that I was going out and to keep the door locked as I would be late coming home, and with that I went out into the heavy, constant rain and walked purposefully to my car as I set out on a very special journey.

It took around twenty minutes for me to drive to Larkhall and by the time I arrived the rain had eased off. It was around 10 p.m. and dusk. I grabbed the torch from the back seat as I climbed from my car and made the dark, eerie walk to the estate. I knew Broomhill better than I knew my own house, but the years since I had last been there had been unkind to the old place. It was overgrown and unkempt and as I made my way closer to the site of the house I saw a burned-out, overturned car in what would have been one of the back rooms of the once stately home. I crunched broken glass and empty cans into the grass underfoot and saw a pile of large stones sticking up through the grass; the remnants of Broomhill House. The adrenalin was running through my veins and I knew I was putting myself in an unsafe situation, and not just because of The Black Lady, but in that moment I didn't care. This had to be done.

I slowly made my way to what would have been the front

of the property, overlooking the glen and the awesome view, as the sun set on the horizon. A small section of the front exterior wall, no more than three feet high, was still standing, although it was daubed by indecipherable graffiti. I ran my hand over the top of the wall and looked out across the pitch-black glen, memories filling my head.

I walked along a well-worn path round the side of the piles of boulders and broken walls, squeezing past bushes and ducking under hanging tree branches. I saw small scorch marks in the grass, remnants of small fires probably made by drinkers to keep warm while they consumed their carry-outs. It appeared that the estate was now a drinking den but tonight it seemed the coast was clear, the earlier weather probably putting any visitors off. It wasn't the living that particularly concerned me, for now anyway.

I collected some dried wood and constructed a small mound from it as darkness fell. I brought a lighter from my pocket and lit the wood using some dried grass as kindling, and then lit a cigarette. Time became inconsequential but I know I spent a couple of hours there, night into morning, Friday into Saturday, and although I did not see her, eventually I felt her presence.

I did an exorcism; the first in a long, long time. And immediately I could feel the change. Everything was calm in that moment. There was no sound, no wind, and no rain. It was just The Black Lady and me. And then it was just me.

It was peaceful. I felt a fresh breeze on my face that I just wanted to breathe in deeply. It was a lovely, almost scented breeze that seemed to be swirling around my head. Abruptly, it stopped and I knew then she was gone. She was away and I hoped, despite it all, that she was finally happy. She was free again, no longer earthbound, and in that moment I believed that was what she was searching for all along.

I collected my belongings, extinguished the fire and slowly followed a path back to my car. I was exhausted and it took all of my remaining strength to walk the distance. I travelled home in silence, switching off the radio as I turned the key in the ignition. The roads were quiet, only the occasional passing lorry and its powerful headlights interrupting the darkness around me. I turned into my driveway, driving ever so slowly to ensure I wouldn't wake my greyhounds in the kennels at the rear of the house and turned off the engine and lights, easing myself gently out of the car.

I staggered into the house and removed my coat, discarding it over the back of a chair in the living room. I switched on a lamp and sat down to remove my boots. I took a few deep breaths and waited for this feeling to pass, and then brought out my mobile phone, punched in the telephone number of a friend, and listened as the answer phone message told me to speak after the beep.

'I'm just back from Broomhill House. It's a little after 1 a.m. It's finished. The Black Lady's gone.'

I hung up and placed the phone on the table beside me and leaned back in the chair. In the seventy-first year of my life, could the woman who first came to me when I was seven years old finally be gone?

I believed she was but I had been wrong before. If she wasn't really gone how long would she wait before revealing herself to me again . . . and how would she do it?

As the familiar sound of the returning rain filled the silence, my eyes flickered shut with uneasy, disturbing thoughts filling my mind.

2

The Maid of the Glen

I sat in the passenger seat of the estate car, the plush leather interior hot to touch in the basking July sunshine, as McGregor drove along the long and winding A82, his window rolled down and his long hair fluttering lightly in the wind. The stunning scenery was all-encompassing and seemingly never-ending; beautiful shades of green from the thousands of trees, the lochs' blue water sparkling so much under the bright sunlight that it dazzled the eyes, and shadows cast by the sprawling hills.

It was the evening of Sunday, 22 July 1962, and we were on our way to a hamlet in Argyll and Bute called Achindarroch; a place so small that it wasn't even listed on many road maps. We were nearing the end of the three-hour drive from Larkhall, as was indicated by the dominant and harsh beauty of the hills of Glencoe, one of the most awe-inspiring sights in Britain and a visual reminder of just how tiny we really are in this world. Achindarroch was just a short distance beyond here, on the west coast of Scotland halfway between Fort William and Oban and within spitting distance of Loch Linnhe.

It was proving to be our busiest year yet. It was only a week since I had appeared on a new Scottish Television Saturday night programme called *Late Night Final* and it was just a few

A long distance view of Loch Linnhe from the mouth of Glen Duror forest, which overlooks Achindarroch, near Glencoe.

months before my appearance on BBC's *Tonight* show, when I tried to exorcise the Black Lady of Broomhill House in front of the television cameras. This ongoing nationwide exposure had led to further interest in our work and now the letters were arriving almost daily. Not all of them were from terrified individuals who feared they were being haunted by an unknown spectre; many of the notes were to tell us about legends and sightings in various locations around the country, with the suggestion we investigate in an attempt to uncover the full story.

We didn't have time to look into every case but one such letter had piqued McGregor's interest and now, weeks on, we had found enough time to make the long drive and camp overnight in Achindarroch to investigate the claims.

The subject of the unsigned letter was 'The Maid of the

Glen', said to be the oft-sighted spirit of a maid that roamed the village and specifically Ben Vair, which loomed over the sparsely populated area. The glen part of the ghost's name was in reference to Glen Duror, a nearby forest.

The letter explained that the maid was a young lady believed to be called Flora MacColl, who had, in an undetermined moment in time – perhaps even centuries before – attempted to go to the rescue of a ship that had foundered in the high seas during a storm. Why she went out on a rowing boat alone in such conditions is unknown, not to mention how odd it might seem that a woman rather than a man would attempt a rescue mission in those bygone days, but row out she did with dogged determination. She located some of the survivors and pulled the spluttering, shocked men onto her boat and took them to shore. No sooner had she helped them onto land than

The loch at dusk, this is where the Maid of the Glen drowned as she attempted to rescue stricken sailors.

she was pushing the fragile vessel back out to sea, focused only on rescuing as many of the stricken sailors as she could before it was too late. It is believed she completed another rescue journey before her third attempt proved one trip too many and her boat capsized amidst truly treacherous conditions, drowning the heroic maid.

Not too long after her death, the image of a young lady wearing clothing traditional to a maid – loose-fitting shirt, long skirt and a cap – was spotted floating across the glen, the grazing fields near to the local farmhouse and even up on Ben Vair. A rumour began circulating in the area that a bowl of porridge was being left outside to the rear of the farm each night and by morning the bowl was empty.

As I sat in McGregor's opulent office listening to him read the letter, I wondered why food would be left for a ghost since they don't need to eat, but the next section of the note perhaps went someway to providing an explanation. It recounted two stories from recent years that had, to our knowledge, never received widespread publicity but, if true, certainly should have done.

The first told the tale of the discovery of an RAF fighter plane that had gone down in Glen Duror during the war. No remains of the pilot could be found amongst the wreckage but that was because, upon impact, and as the pilot struggled from the debris, a female figure had appeared before him and beckoned him to follow. No doubt thinking he had died and was now in the spirit world, the pilot stumbled after the pretty, fair-haired young woman as she led him to a cave. He later claimed that she fed him porridge and cared for him until he had enough strength to walk to the local police station.

The second account was in a similar vein and happened just a couple of years after the pilot's experience. It's a Hansel and

Gretel-esque story except that the lady in the woods had honour-able intentions. Two children became lost while playing in the forest and a search by locals proved fruitless, but this was because the children had met a mute lady, dressed like a maid, who guided them to a cave where she fed and nurtured them, before pointing the boy and girl in the right direction out of the woods.

The letter writer backed up many of his claims by pointing McGregor towards a book, should he be able to find a copy, that he said made mention of the Maid of the Glen. My mentor turned round and gazed from floor to ceiling at the long rows of books that would make any public library green with envy, then ran his thumb along one section in particular until he located the book in question; a lime-coloured hardback with gold lettering. He flicked through the dusty pages until he came to the section on the Maid and nodded his head in approval as he read the brief passage aloud.

So, here we were in the uncomfortably warm and sticky July heat; just myself, McGregor and, sitting in the backseat, the newest and final member of our unique gang, Willie. I had known the Motherwell lad, who was five or six years older than me, for a long time, having first met him through work where we became good friends.

I introduced him to McGregor after Johnny asked if I knew anyone who could do some repair work around his house. I immediately thought of Willie, who could turn his hand to anything. For example, many years after this Willie fixed a loom for McGregor, allowing my mentor to fulfil orders for a number of oversized wall carpet hangings. On a trip to Britain several years later, US President Ronald Reagan visited a building where one of McGregor's designs was on display and he was so impressed by it that he wanted one for himself. McGregor was contacted and he set to work on the presidential weave. Sometime later, after he had sent the hanging across the Atlantic, he received a letter from the White House thanking him for the beautiful piece, which had pride of place in one of the president's favourite rooms.

Willie became part of our team soon after first meeting McGregor, as we realised his skills could be advantageous. He proved us right and quickly became indispensable.

He was a strong, wily man, small in stature but big in talent. He was quiet and didn't care for the publicity that often accompanied our line of work, so he gladly stood in the shadows while I, and occasionally McGregor, dealt with the media. Above all, Willie was, quite simply, a genius.

He could make anything imaginable using minimal tools and his bare hands. At the same time as Ian Fleming was writing James Bond books and inventing seemingly outlandish gadgets for Q to give to 007, Willie was doing it for real. He was a man of ideas and creations years ahead of his time and as the three of us gelled and formed a formidable team, we became, without using hyperbole, a group of truly extraordinary gentlemen.

Willie made me a camera from an old wristwatch soon after he joined our gang; not a camera made from watch parts, but an actual camera that was once a working watch and still looked like a working watch. It came complete with a range finder on the watch face where the date slot used to be. He knew that strange occurrences tended to happen in my presence, so he created this device so I always had a camera to hand should something show itself to me. The mini camera only had capacity for two frames owing to its limited size but this was better than nothing in an emergency situation.

This trip to Achindarroch wasn't Willie's first job with us

although at this stage he had only been a part of the team for a few months. He had yet to develop and invent many of the tools we would take on our investigations, although he did bring along one accessory he had made just days before; a guitar he had constructed from an old tea chest. A week before we came on the trip, McGregor said he would bring his button accordion in case we needed to pass the time should the Maid fail to appear. Willie added that he would bring his guitar, to which I said I didn't know he had one.

'I don't,' he told me, 'but I'll make one.'

He went to the local Co-op and asked if they had any of the wooden chests that the loose tea was delivered in back in those days and, within the week, Willie had made a guitar that looked and sounded great.

The accordion and homemade guitar lay in the spacious boot beside the three-man tent as we drove into Clan Stewart of Appin country, the rugged and remote district that is surrounded and intercepted by vast lochs, flowing rivers and looming hills. It's also the site of one of Scotland's most infamous murder cases.

The Clan Stewart of Appin, or The Loyal Clan, has been regarded as a separate clan since the fifteenth century and were faithful supporters of the Jacobite cause. In May 1752, a government agent called Colin Campbell of Glenure, better know as The Red Fox, travelled to Glen Duror under the pretence of collecting taxes, but in reality he was going to evict the Stewarts of Appin from their homes to make way for the government-loyal Campbells. As he and his small group of men approached Ballachulish Bridge, he was shot and killed. The chief suspect, Alan Breck Stewart, fled to France but justice had to be seen to be done so a fellow Stewart known as James of the Glen – who had a cast iron alibi for the time of the murder – was tried and found guilty in a sham trial at Inverary. Eleven of the jurors were Campbells and one of the three judges was the Duke of Argyll, head of the Campbell clan.

James was hanged near to the spot where The Red Fox was murdered and his body left to rot for eighteen months, the decomposing shell swaying in the wind as a crass symbol of retribution and an eye for an eye justice. The incident was immortalised thanks to Robert Louis Stevenson, who incorporated the episode and based a main character on Alan Breck in his classic novel, *Kidnapped*.

As a footnote, nearly 250 years later in 2001, a descendant of the Stewarts of Appin broke the clan's long silence on the matter and apparently divulged the real murderer's identity. Anda Penman, an eighty-nine-year-old woman claimed, in her dying days, that four young Stewart men had planned the murder and Donald Stewart of Ballachulish fired the fatal shot. Anda died soon after and no other Stewart has backed up her claims, so whether this is the definitive statement on the matter is questionable.

We could feel the bloody history of the area as we made our way into Achindarroch and quickly located the property in question, a typical looking farmhouse of white painted, heavy stone with outhouses to the rear and sprawling fields stretching into the distance towards the hills. We parked the car next to the tractor at the side of the house and McGregor approached to knock on the door while we stood back. We didn't want to alarm the inhabitants by opening the door to find three strangers standing there.

The door opened and an elderly man appeared before McGregor.

'Hello there, sir, my name is John McGregor and these two

men with me,' he said, turning and pointing towards us, 'are my colleagues, Tom and Willie. We've travelled through from Lanarkshire this fine evening and I'll tell you why we've turned up at your door unannounced. We received an anonymous letter telling us about someone called the Maid of the Glen, who you might have heard of?'

The old gentlemen's eyes widened and he smiled a little.

'Aye, we've all heard tell of the Maid around these parts. I cannae say for sure where you'll find her, though.'

'Well, sir, you see, we're actually well versed in these matters. We investigate claims of ghosts and strange happenings around the country and we'd like to spend the night in Achindarroch to see if we might happen to come across the Maid. We wondered if you would be so kind to allow us to set up our tent in the field behind your house for the evening.'

The old man looked us over and then stepped to the side.

'Come in, lads, and have a cup of tea with my wife and me. What you're asking shouldn't be a problem, I don't think.'

We followed him in and Willie closed the door. We joined him in the living room, which was sparsely furnished and decorated but homely, as he explained to the sprightly looking woman sitting in a firm, high-backed wooden chair by the fireplace, who we were and what we had requested.

We exchanged pleasantries as she stood and walked to the kitchen, where she filled a kettle and placed it on the stove. She brought five mismatched cups from a cupboard and sat them on the sideboard while she chatted to us. Once the kettle was boiled and the tea poured, we went back into the living room, where I began asking questions about the Maid.

They both looked at each other before admitting they had seen what the locals referred to as the Maid of the Glen.

'We've seen her away out at the back of the field, heading

towards the hills,' she said. 'Never up close but aye, we've seen her.'

'We know she's not human because she glides, if you understand,' her husband added. 'She doesn't walk like a normal person. There's space between where she ends and the ground begins, and as far as I can make out she's wearing helluva old-fashioned clothes.'

'Do you see where she goes?' Willie asked.

'Up into the hills. She disappears into the distance. Not disappears like one minute she's there and the next she's not, just that she's too far away to see,' he replied. 'Some say she has a cave up in the hills.'

'Aye, we've heard a couple of those stories, too,' I said.

Before we had set out on the trip we had discussed whether we should look for the cave but Appin is awash with such fissures and there was no way of determining which one it might be. Majestically titled caves such as the Cave of Broken Expectations, Cave of the Voices and one of Scotland's deepest caves, the Cave of Skulls, which was only discovered in 1999, dominate the area but probably the most likely candidate for the Maid's bolthole was Ardsheal's Cave.

Located on Ben Vair, itself said to be named after a dragon, the cave was the hiding place for Charles Stewart of Ardsheal, one of Bonnie Prince Charlie's commanding officers. After the defeat at Culloden, Stewart went on the run from the English Red Coats and hid in the cave for a long time. His hideaway was so successful owing to a waterfall that completely hides the entrance, so unless one knew the exact location, the cave's opening might never be discovered.

'What about the story we've heard about a bowl of porridge being left out every night, supposedly for the Maid?' I asked.

'We know nothing about that,' the man quickly replied. 'Not

a thing. If that happened it must have been done years ago, well before our time here.'

The chat continued for a few more minutes until the old man excused himself and said there was something he had to check on outside. His wife continued to pass the time with us until he came back, where he said he had bumped into the forestry commissioner, whose property line bordered the farmland. We were informed he would be willing to talk with us, too. I had a feeling it was a polite way of telling us our time was up, so we sat down the empty cups and made our way outside. The middle-aged, burly forestry man was pottering around on his property as we approached him. There was a woman with him, who I presumed was his wife.

We went across and reached over the low wire fence to introduce ourselves. For someone who was happy to talk to us he was strangely uncommunicative, and his female companion wasn't any better. After a short, strained conversation, we learned that they had heard reports of a woman spotted in the fields but they hadn't seen her and weren't prepared to say any more about the matter. Cutting our losses, we thanked them for their time and returned to the car to retrieve what we needed for the night. While McGregor and Willie carried the tent and sleeping bags to the field behind the farmhouse, I knocked on the old couple's door and presented the gentleman with an unopened bottle of whisky I had in my holdall as a thank you for his hospitality and for allowing us to pitch our tent on his property.

By the time I made my way over to my two pals, the tent was already taking shape. We were around twenty to thirty feet from the house in the empty grazing field, where the grass was short and thankfully free from any farm animals at this time. The only other thing in the field that I could see was an old

The field where Tom, McGregor and Willie spent the night in search of the Maid of the Glen, who appeared to them before disappearing into the trees. Glen Duror towers over the landscape.

bath located farther up from the tent, which I presumed was there as a trough for when animals were kept here. The sun was going down behind the vast, foreboding hill that loomed over us, its peak hidden by a white, fluffy cloud, as we hammered the pegs into the firm ground. By the time we were finished and had laid blankets down inside the spacious tent it was dusk and the sky was a kaleidoscope of colours. We were in a stunning part of Scotland on a warm summer's night and it served as a reminder of how lucky we were to live in such a beautiful country.

I picked up one of the three torches we had in the holdall and switched it on to make sure it was working, in case we needed it during the night. The light from the torch lit up the ground at my feet and I pointed it all around me to check its reach. Willie had tinkered with the torches in a bid to make the beams more powerful and far-reaching and, as usual, he had succeeded.

As I shone the torch, the light flashed over an object that caught my attention. I walked back towards the farmhouse, covering my hand over the torch so only a small speck of light escaped, just enough to guide me. The house was in darkness so I was careful not to make a noise as I approached the window, which I hoped wasn't the couple's bedroom for fear they might hear me. On the sill was a bowl, with another bowl upturned and placed on top, which I carefully removed and placed aside the other one while gripping the torch under my oxter. I bent down under the window with the second bowl in my hand and shone the torchlight onto it. I shook my head and smiled, put the bowls back how I had found them and slipped quietly back to camp.

'What were you doing?' McGregor asked as I crawled inside the tent, his accordion by his side.

'There's a bowl of porridge sitting on the windowsill down there. They've covered it up with another bowl. It was still warm. I could feel the heat from it.'

'They must've put it out the window while we were setting up the tent. Did they think we wouldn't notice?' Willie added.

'Maybe they thought they could put it out and retrieve it in the morning without us seeing,' McGregor said. 'It's obviously a ritual they have. We all know that ghosts don't eat, so what's it for? Whatever's going on, we know they've lied to us about this so they might have been lying about other things, too, so we stay alert at all times.'

McGregor's accordion and Willie's homemade guitar remained untouched on the tartan blanket in order to make sure we didn't miss any sudden noises or movements. We lit a candle which we secured on a saucer with hot wax and placed on a tiny plastic table to give it a little height, but not too much that it might set the tent on fire. I brought out my bible, which I'd had since my Sunday School days, and placed it unopened on the blanket next to the table. In those days I always carried a bible on our investigations; it wouldn't make any evil spirits vanish the moment I opened it, but neither could it do any harm. All it could do was good and perhaps offer help and guidance should we need an edge.

We chatted quietly as the hours ticked by and night stretched into early morning. It was so peaceful with not even a hint of wind outside; a hot, humid summer's night.

Time went on and McGregor lay on top of his sleeping bag reading a book, while I sat cross-legged playing patience and Willie sketched his latest invention or modification on a scrap of paper using a bookies' pencil I'd given him.

Suddenly it all changed. I placed the deck of cards down and looked at my exposed forearms; the hairs were standing on end. There was something out there. I could feel the atmosphere alter in that moment. I turned round to look at McGregor but he was already staring at me; he'd noticed my expression change and was throwing down his book and reaching for the torches before I'd even opened my mouth to alert them. Willie was aware something was happening now, too, and we were all on our haunches ready to climb out of the tent within seconds of me feeling the presence.

I scrambled out first, torch in hand, and the others followed. It was dark outside, obviously, but not pitch dark. I don't think the sky ever truly blackens in the Highlands during summer nights as calm and peaceful as that one, instead it was an almost glowing purple hue. Some people say this is thanks to the heather but I don't know about that.

I looked around but could only see the dark and darker shapes of inanimate objects; the outhouses to my left, the old bath beyond the tent, the fence that separated the field from the forestry commissioner's land, the trees and bushes in the distance. Willie and McGregor were by my side and throwing fleeting glances all over the area.

'Do you see anything?' McGregor whispered.

'No. Come on, let's spread out and keep our eyes peeled,' I responded. I walked slowly towards the far side while McGregor went up the middle and Willie the opposite side. As I moved, the feeling started to fade and I realised I was on the wrong track so I turned back and crossed the field, passing by the tent. The feeling grew stronger again. Willie was ahead of me so I whispered over to McGregor to join us on this side, next to the wire fence that separated our grazing field with the forestry land. I switched on my torch and directed it over the fence; there was what appeared to be a shallow gully running parallel to the fence, perhaps for drainage purposes, and then long, almost hay-like grass that was waist height. Farther ahead there was a line of pine trees, which eventually formed into a huge cluster as the ground on both sides of the fence inclined before leading to an impenetrable blanket of trees at the foot of the hill.

I leaned on a fence post and looked into the adjoining land. I could see a shape; a human shape.

I shone the torch in its direction and suddenly she was there, around thirty feet from us, in the gully.

The Maid of the Glen.

She had been watching us, but the moment the light was directed at her she turned and moved away. In the split second I had to see her face I could tell she had been young, almost youthful in appearance. She had long hair, some of which was covered with an old-fashioned cap, and wore a green jacket or shawl and a white, wide, pleated long skirt.

She was a strong spirit. I was certain of that, because I couldn't see through her clear image. Were it not for the empty space between the bottom of her flowing skirt and the ground then it may have been hard for some people to tell she was no longer a living person.

I put my foot on the wire fence as it buckled and wobbled under my weight, and hopped over and into the gully.

I pointed the torch to the ground to ensure I didn't stumble into any holes or over any fallen branches, but the noise behind me indicated one of my mates hadn't been so lucky. I looked round to see Willie lying on the ground in a heap after his trailing leg had caught on the fence. He ignored whatever pain he was feeling and scrambled to his feet as we turned our attention back to the Maid, who was stealing a march on us.

In single file the three of us rushed after the ghost, the three beams from the torches bouncing up and down on the ground like malfunctioning disco lights in conjunction with our heavy steps. We moved from a trot to a sprint as we attempted to keep her in our sights. She was now only around twenty feet ahead of us.

Suddenly she pulled away again and I asked myself, as the beads of sweat formed on my brow, if she was playing a game. She could disappear whenever she wanted, but here we were, running along a ditch in the dead of night with the long grass brushing against our chests, chasing after this spirit. Maybe it was the hot, balmy weather that had made us react in such a fashion or, dare I say, we had been caught up in the moment. We hadn't even lifted the camera before we gave chase, in a bid to gain a better glimpse of the Maid.

She glided with ease, looking straight ahead all the way. We huffed and puffed up the steady incline as the going underfoot became rougher and more treacherous. The sound of the dead branches snapping underfoot and the swishing of the long grass rubbing against our clothes amplified and carried across the fields until it sounded like it was coming from afar.

Maybe she wanted us to follow her, I thought. But no sooner had those words passed through my head than she vanished as she approached the wall of trees up ahead. We came to a halt and all three of us gasped for air.

'She's away, lads,' McGregor wheezed after a moment. 'She's gone.' Willie and I nodded in forlorn agreement. I wiped my brow with my shirtsleeve and turned round to face camp.

It wasn't hard to see because the tent was glowing.

'Did we leave the candle lit, boys?' I asked, pointing towards the tent in the distance.

'Christ, we must've, Tom,' Willie answered. 'The whole lot could have gone up in flames if the candle had fallen over.'

'Aye, you're right but do you know what? I can't remember seeing the light before now. I walked by the tent when we started looking for the Maid and I don't remember noticing the glow,' I responded.

We walked down the slope towards camp with renewed purpose.

'You were distracted, though. We all were. We weren't paying any attention to the tent and it might not have registered at the time even if we did notice,' McGregor reasoned.

At the fence, one of us shone the light on the wire while the others clambered over, taking care this time to ensure we each made it to the other side without incident. I switched off my torch as I reached the tent and hunched down in order to crawl inside.

At first everything seemed fine. But then I looked closer and my heart started thumping once again.

'Budge over a wee bit, Tom, we can't get in.' Willie was at my heels but my brain barely registered his statement. The two sights before me consumed my attention.

I crawled over to the small plastic table in the centre of the tent where the candle and saucer had been placed. On that saucer the dripping wax had formed into a perfectly formed heart shape, around two inches square. It was as if it had been moulded or cast, except it was still attached to the base of the candle.

I was leaning in so close to the flame to study the heart that I could feel the heat on the side of my face and when I blinked all I could see was the yellow flicker of the candlelight.

As Willie and McGregor struggled into the tent, I pointed to the saucer before they had the chance to say anything, while I picked up the bible that I'd left closed beside the table. Except now the bible was open.

Maybe it was a fluke or coincidence or perhaps I was drawn to it for a reason, but my eyes fixed on a verse on the page: 'But Jesus called them unto him, and said, "Suffer little children to come unto me, and forbid them not: for of such is the kingdom of God."' Chapter eighteen, verse sixteen from the book of . . . I looked to the top of the page for confirmation . . . Luke.

'Would you look at that, Johnny. That's amazing,' I heard Willie exclaim. He was rubbing shoulders with me but his voice sounded a million miles away as I stared at the yellow-tipped pages of the worn bible in my hands.

The story of the Maid sheltering and caring for the lost children sprang to mind and I wondered if she was trying to send a message. Was there a connection between the wax heart and bible verse?

'What's caught your attention there, Tom?' McGregor had moved round beside me as Willie continued to examine the candle.

'The bible was opened when I came back.'

'Are you sure it was closed before we went out?'

'Definitely. When I picked it up this verse seemed to jump out at me.' I read it to him. 'Any ideas?'

'Well, Jesus is saying there that it's people like these children, good and loving, that he wants in his kingdom. This was after the disciples had begun turning the kids away when a long line of parents brought them to be blessed.'

'So, what's she trying to tell us? You don't think she's trying to pass on a message from heaven, do you?'

'I don't know. Maybe it correlates with the heart.'

'That's what I was thinking, too.'

Willie had been listening to the conversation even if he didn't appear to be as he softly prodded and poked at the wax shape.

'The bible falling open, you could accept as a fluke. The wax forming into this heart shape . . . it's highly irregular and unlikely but I'll be devil's advocate and say it could be a one-in-a-million coincidence. Both occurring at the same time, in the same place? No way,' Willie offered.

There was a prolonged moment of silence while we tried to digest it all, and then Willie asked one of us to point a torch towards the candle. He blew out the flame and brought out a pocketknife and gently sliced and slid the heart from the base of the candle and off the saucer into the palm of his hand. He reached into his bag and pulled out a cloth or a t-shirt and carefully wrapped the wax inside the material.

Willie would later cut and shape two pieces of Perspex into the shape of the heart, which he placed inside the plastic and sealed shut. He presented it to McGregor as a keepsake and memento of our adventures and John kept it until his dying day. Maybe it's still out there somewhere, I don't know. I hope it is.

Willie relit the candle and reached for his pipe while he had the matches to hand. McGregor followed suit and while I was never too fond of the pipe, a cigarette seemed like a good idea right then.

Goodness knows how much time passed by as we sat in the tent discussing in detail all that had come before. We had been shocked, and that wasn't easy to do, let me tell you. We each took a turn to recount the night's events and found we were in complete agreement about how it had played out.

Eventually our tiredness was overpowering and we drifted off to sleep. The candle's flame flickered and died and the light went out over the opened bible on the centre of the floor.

I couldn't have been sleeping for any more than two hours when the morning light and the sound of birds woke me from the incongruous, twisted position in which I'd fallen asleep. I stretched my arms behind my head and rubbed my aching neck as my eyes once again locked in on the bible by my feet.

I slowly crawled out of the tent and squinted until I became accustomed to the bright sunlight. It was barely 5 a.m. and I doubted the old couple in the farmhouse would be out of their bed yet, so I walked down to the cottage to check on the bowls sitting on the windowsill.

I gently lifted the one that was upturned and, sure enough, the bowl underneath was empty.

The porridge was gone; not so much as a sticky crumb remained.

I placed the crockery back the way I had found it and walked away, shaking my head.

I didn't understand this at all. Ghosts do not eat. But then again, the Maid had proved itself to be no ordinary ghost; a rather oxymoronic statement, I realise.

I had no idea. Willie and McGregor were nonplussed about it, too. We agreed it was time to go; we would dismantle the tent and make a start on the long journey, stopping somewhere around Glencoe for breakfast.

I always carried a bar of soap and a towel with me, no matter where I was going to be camping, so I could freshen myself up after a night under canvas. I looked around for a source of water and could see only one thing – the bath-cum-trough.

Why not? I thought. There weren't any animals in the field so if it looked clean and fresh it would do the trick. I collected the soap and towel from my bag and walked over to the old bath. It was surprisingly clean and half filled with water, into which I dipped my hand, finding it to be pleasantly lukewarm. I removed my shirt and plunged my hands and the soap into the water and worked up a lather, but no sooner had I begun washing than I felt a sharp pain in my shoulder that made me flinch. Then there was a twinge in my forearm and a pang in my chest and I looked down to see a red mark protruding through the soapsuds on my skin. Suddenly, I had an un-controllable itch and I realised I was being eaten alive by some sort of bug, maybe the dreaded Scottish midge. But if it was, then these must have been mutant midges because the bites were huge. I towelled myself down and rushed back to base, pulling on my shirt and scratching incessantly like a dog with fleas.

We pulled down the tent in haste, collected our belongings and loaded the bags and ourselves into the car. It was time to go.

On the way home we decided our night in Achindarroch

had thrown up more questions than answers and a return trip was more than merited. We vowed to come back, a promise echoed through the pages of the *Daily Express* just two days later under the headline, 'BIG TOM TELLS HOW HE CHASED THE MAID'.

But sometimes promises are broken. We never did return to Achindarroch in search of the Maid and the porridge paradox, but the reason for our no show is worth explaining.

The name Colonel Percy Harrison Fawcett may not be instantly recognisable to most people nowadays, but at one time it was familiar to many.

Colonel Fawcett was a British archaeologist and explorer born in Torquay in 1867. He was a friend of the legendary authors Sir H. Rider Haggard and Sir Arthur Conan Doyle and it is rumoured that Indiana Jones was based on Fawcett. He was invited by the Royal Geographic Society to go on an expedition to South America in 1906, to map a jungle area and establish borders between Brazil and Bolivia.

It was the first of several explorations but the adventurer, who had a strong interest in the occult and telepathy, set out on his final journey in 1925 when he, along with his eldest son Jack and Jack's friend Raleigh Rimmell, received financing to go in search of an ancient lost city, known simply as Z, which he believed to exist in the Mato Grosso region.

The final correspondence from Fawcett or his companions came on 29 May 1925, when he sent a telegraph to his wife, Nina, which stated he was about to go into unexplored territory with the two boys. 'You need have no fear of failure . . .' were his last recorded words.

Many theories were presented over the years: natives had killed him, local tribesmen took him hostage, he suffered amnesia, a giant anaconda attacked him . . . even that he had actually found the lost city.

Subsequently, more than 100 supposed explorers and heroic rescuers have died over the course of thirteen expeditions in an attempt to uncover Fawcett's fate, even though he stated resolutely that he wished no one to come after him should he fail in his mission.

We wanted a big challenge and, with our profile at its peak, it looked like our ambitions would be realised when we were offered financial backing to stage our own exploration and search for Fawcett, although truth be told we were more interested in discovering the city of Z. Fawcett was the big deal for the public, so when we were dealing with the potential backers we talked about searching for the Colonel, when really it was the ancient city we sought. If Fawcett had found his El Dorado, we might have been lucky enough to discover both at the same time.

As the likelihood of our trip increased, McGregor would often recite the final verse of Edgar Allen Poe's poem 'El Dorado' to Willie and me:

> 'Over the Mountains
> Of the Moon,
> Down the Valley of the Shadow,
> Ride, boldly ride,'
> The shade replied –
> 'If you seek for El Dorado.'

We planned every minute detail and the multi-lingual McGregor brushed up on his Portuguese and Spanish over the course of the next several months as discussions with a group of backers, led by a main financier, continued. The papers got wind of the trip and we were all over the broadsheets, which we hoped would increase our chances of receiving the necessary financial support.

We were dreaming of finding our Shangri-La when suddenly we came crashing back to normality with a sickening and sudden thump. For undisclosed reasons the financial deal collapsed before any contracts could be signed and that was that . . . the dream was over.

It was a hard one to take and we were all extremely disappointed, especially after such a long and protracted journey that had brought us to this insurmountable block in the road.

Our heads dropped for a while, I admit; there would be something wrong if they didn't, but one evening while we sat in McGregor's office I picked up the pile of recently delivered letters and said to my comrades:

'Look at this right here. In every one of these envelopes is the potential for another great adventure. Let's give ourselves a shake and get started.'

That's exactly what we did and I was right, there were plenty more unbelievable adventures in the months and years ahead.

As for Fawcett . . . well, it's still unknown where his final resting place may be or the fate that befell him. The Maid of the Glen, on the other hand, I know exactly where she is. And if I ever make it back to Achindarroch, I dare say I might come face-to-face with her one more time.

3

No Salvation Required

Not all spooky stories end with the discovery of a ghost.

Quite often people refuse to believe that the strange occurrences or odd phenomena that are disturbing their lives could be linked to the paranormal. Then there are those people who are scared witless and are too quick to blame it on a haunting or something otherworldly.

Let me tell you a story where not everything was as it seemed, where the answer came to me in a fish and chip shop, and where I delivered the improbable, but not out-of-this-world, explanation before my Sunday tea was cold.

I married Margaret when I was twenty-five after a three-year engagement. She was five years my junior and we were married in the local church in Larkhall, followed by a reception in the town's Co-operative Hall where all our family and friends tucked into a lovely steak pie meal. It was a momentous March day, not only was I marrying my sweetheart but it was the biggest date in the horse racing calendar, the day of The Grand National, and there was a horse running by the name of Wyndburgh on which I never failed to bet.

The horse has since gone down in Grand National history

as the only runner to finish second three times – in 1957, 1959 and 1962 – and never win. The second of its three runner-up finishes was all the more remarkable since one of the stirrup irons belonging to Wyndburgh's jockey, Tim Brookshaw, broke at Becher's Brook on the second circuit and he rode the rest of the way without any stirrups.

However, Wyndburgh wasn't even to get a placed finish on my wedding day, as it fell just after the race began. But regardless of the race's outcome I was still quids in that day, as I wedded the woman I loved.

Once we were married we moved from Larkhall to nearby Motherwell, a larger, more bustling town. It was known as the steel production capital of Scotland and was even referred to as Steelopolis, largely due to the huge site known as Ravenscraig. Work on the steelworks started in 1954 and, by the time Margaret and I moved to the town, it was the provider of hundreds of jobs for the local area. The familiar sight of the blue water tower was synonymous with the Motherwell skyline for decades, until the site closed and it was eventually demolished in the early 1990s.

We rented an upstairs flat in a cul-de-sac called Macdonald Street, just off one of the town's main thoroughfares of old red sandstone buildings. I was working hard every day and enjoyed coming in each night to Margaret's lovely home-cooked meals. The aroma of the food would strike my senses the moment I opened the front door and make my stomach rumble in anticipation.

Over such a dinner one evening, Margaret told me of a conversation she had had earlier in the day with another couple we had befriended in the street. Paul and Linda stayed in the ground floor flat of the gable-end house but Linda confided in Margaret that they were becoming increasingly scared of living there, as they feared they had a ghost. They knew what I did in my spare time but Linda had told Margaret they didn't want to approach me directly in case I thought they were having a joke at my expense.

After my meal I pulled on my shoes and jacket and walked the couple of blocks to Paul's flat. They invited me in and I asked what was troubling them. Paul told me they could hear accordion music coming from within the house, at least once a week. At first, they thought it might have been one of their neighbours but had asked around and discovered nobody played the accordion. More interestingly, no one else had been hearing the music. Linda told me it was loudest in the bedroom so, with their permission, I went into the room and looked around. Nothing seemed out of the ordinary on first glance.

The reason they feared a supernatural presence was quite simple and completely understandable.

The old gentleman who had lived in the flat before them was a great accordion player and often played at local events. When he died he was found lying on his bed, in what was now Paul and Linda's room, with the button-key accordion strapped to his front. It was estimated he had been lying like that for three or four days before he was discovered.

I, too, was aware of the story and with that in mind, I told Paul and Linda to give me a shout the next time they heard the music and I would come straight over.

I didn't have too long to wait. True to my word, I went straight to their house and as Linda opened the door and I stepped inside, a tune became faintly audible. I walked along the hallway and with every step I took the sound increased. I told Paul and Linda, who stood behind me in nervous antici-pation, that I could hear the music and, yes, it did sound like an accordion.

I stood still in the centre of the living room, my head cocked to the side like a dog attempting to understand its master. It wasn't unbearably loud but it was certainly loud enough to cause a distraction.

'You're certain no one in the block plays the accordion or even listens to accordion records?' I asked.

'Well, I've asked each of our neighbours and they've assured me they don't. I've no reason to believe they would lie to me,' Paul replied. 'Come into the bedroom. It's even louder there.'

I followed Paul into the room and Linda walked behind me. He was right. It was louder. I walked round the bedroom slowly, moving between the furniture and stopping occasionally as I tried to place the name of the tune being played.

However, something didn't seem right. On this occasion, I didn't have the feeling I have when a presence is nearby. That concerned me and raised a doubt in my mind that the spirit of the old accordion player wasn't the source of the music. Perhaps there was a more straightforward explanation but I could not hazard a guess as to what that might be.

Paul and Linda's house was situated on the corner of Macdonald Street and Camp Street, the road adjacent to our cul-de-sac. Camp Street was a main road on a steep hill, over which the couple's living room window looked out. On the ground floor of the buildings in this area was a trapdoor, which led down to a crawl space.

I asked Paul where the trap door was in his flat and he told me it was where we were standing right now, in the bedroom. I shuffled my feet over the carpet until I felt the handle under the soles of my shoes, just below the foot of the bed. Luckily, Paul hadn't tacked the carpet to the floor and the sparse amount of furniture in this section wasn't too heavy, so it was with relative ease that we pulled the carpet back to reveal the trapdoor. I pulled up the handle and looked down into the darkness. He fetched me a torch from the pantry and I shone it into the black hole where I could see nothing untoward, so I lowered myself down into the dusty space for a closer inspection.

It was bigger than your typical crawl space and I was actually able to stand upright thanks to the gradient of the street. It was almost like another room, a cellar. There were some pipes overhead and up the walls, and these ran under each of the houses but I could see nothing unusual. The music was still playing down here, maybe even louder, but still I couldn't see the performer.

Paul helped me back up out of the crawlspace and I dusted myself off.

'I'm not too sure about this,' I admitted to the couple. 'I can hear the music just like you can but I'm not getting that feeling I normally have in these situations, which is worrying me. Let me know when it happens again and I'll come straight back. Maybe I'll have come up with an answer by then.'

Two or three weeks passed without any more calls from Paul or Linda. Early one Sunday evening Margaret asked me to go round to the chip shop on Camp Street and buy a couple of fish suppers for our dinner, as she wanted a well-deserved break from cooking. I would never turn down a fish supper, especially from Davy's chip shop, so I gladly agreed.

I was in the takeaway in next to no time thanks to the gap in the garden railings beside the old washhouses. It was just big enough to allow a person to squeeze through and it led to Camp Street, just next to Davy's. Margaret and I got on well with him and his wife, and I stood in the store chatting with him while he fried my fish.

As we talked I suddenly heard a familiar sound and I lost track of what we were discussing as my mind and ears focused on the music in the distance.

'Davy,' I said, interrupting his chat about football as he shovelled out some chips from the fryer. 'Can you hear that music? Does it sound like an accordion to you?'

He nodded towards the shop entrance and said, 'It's coming from across the road, from the hall over there.' I swivelled round and looked out of the window at the Salvation Army hall across the street.

'Never mind the salt and vinegar, Davy. Just wrap them up and I'll take them as they are, I've got something I need to check.' I handed him the money in exchange for the suppers wrapped in the sports pages of Saturday's newspaper, then turned and walked briskly across the street to the hall, the music becoming louder as I approached the building.

I turned the handle softly and pulled open the door, trying not to make too much noise that might disturb anybody. As I peered into the hall, I saw a Sally Army member sitting at an organ, playing *Onward Christian Soldiers*, as the rest of the congregation sang along.

I stood for a moment watching and then stepped out and closed the door gently behind me. I smiled and shook my head as I walked back across the road towards the gap in the fence. I passed the washhouse and went back inside my house, the mouth-watering smell of the fish and chips filling the kitchen as I handed the parcel to Margaret.

'Give me five minutes. There's something I need to do quickly.'

I didn't give her the chance to question where I was going. I was out of the house and walking towards Paul and Linda's place as quickly as I could. I knocked on their door, slightly out of breath. The door opened and Paul looked surprised to see me standing there.

'How did you know it had started again?' he asked, baffled.

I didn't bother to answer as I went inside and headed towards the bedroom. Linda was there already, looking at the walls as if hoping a hidden answer to where the music was coming from would suddenly appear from the patterned wallpaper.

'Evening, Linda. You don't have a brush or something similar I can borrow for a moment, do you?'

She looked at me a little puzzled, then nodded her head and left the room. I asked Paul to give me a hand pulling back the carpet again and opening the trapdoor to the crawl space. By the time we'd done that Linda was by our sides with a long-handled brush in her grip. She passed it to me. 'Why do you want that?' she asked.

'Do you mind if I take the brush head off just now, Linda, and then I'll show you?' The music was still audible all around us.

She hesitated before saying, 'Aye, alright, I suppose.'

I put my foot on the brush head and pulled the hollow shaft from the brush. I lowered myself down the hole and looked at the pipes running through the basement, as Paul came down behind me. I identified the one I believed to be the water pipe and placed an end of the shaft against it. I held the other end to my ear and listened. There it was . . . clear as a bell. Or in this case, clear as an organ.

'Paul, have a listen. Keep the stick on the pipe and put your ear to this end.' I handed him the shaft and he did as I instructed.

He shook his head. I determined from his furrowed brow and puzzled expression that hearing the music wasn't a problem but understanding the source was.

'It isn't the old man's accordion you've been hearing,' I explained. 'It's an organ. The Salvation Army hall's organ. The distant organ noise sounds similar to an accordion but the music hasn't been coming from inside your house, far from it.'

We climbed out of the crawl space and I returned the pole to Linda, who had the brush head in her hand.

'Now that's your water pipes down there, and they run underneath all the buildings on the street. It's a bit of a freak happening but due to the location of your house, being on the gable end between Camp Street and Macdonald Street, what I think has occurred is the sound of the Salvation Army hall's music has carried along the pipes, bounced up your back wall and been more audible in your home than any other due to its location.'

'My God, Tom, do you think that's what it is?' Linda asked.

'I'm certain of it, Linda,' I replied, brushing the dust off of my jacket. 'So any time they have a band practice or a service, you can hear the music.'

'So it's not the old man's ghost after all?' Paul sighed. 'I feel like an idiot.'

'No, you're ghost-free this time. Don't feel silly, though. Under the circumstances it was a reasonable conclusion to come to and I would probably have thought the same if I was in your shoes. If I hadn't heard the familiar sound while I was standing in Davy's waiting for our dinner then I would still be none the wiser. Speaking of which, I better go before it's cold.'

With that I made my way to the door as Paul and Linda thanked me for solving the mystery of the sound of music. I went home to Margaret, who had my fish supper on a plate waiting for me, and Paul and Linda rested easy in their home, where they spent many happy years together.

They even grew to enjoy the regular music performances that were, quite literally, piped into their flat.

4

Reel to Real: Oscar's Story

Everyone loves a good scare, I was often told, when I would
state I had no interest in going to see a so-called horror film
at the pictures. I had enough chills and close encounters in
real life without sitting in a darkened room as the story on the
big screen tried to terrify me. That wasn't my idea of relaxa-
tion. And it wouldn't have been as frightening as the real thing,
either, let me tell you.

Yet here I was, waiting in the foyer of the Rex cinema in
Motherwell, where I had been told a scare might await me. I
wasn't standing in line waiting to buy a ticket for the latest
Hammer Horror, though. No, I was here because the establishment's manager had requested my presence. I stood to the
side of the ticket booth as patrons filed out the hall, having
just seen the latest Hollywood attraction. They buttoned their
coats and stuffed their hands deep into their pockets as they
left the warmth of the cinema and walked down the four or
five exterior steps of the building into the night air and the
springtime chill.

It was May 1962 and Margaret and I were still living in
Macdonald Street in the Lanarkshire town. Our home was
located just behind Windmillhill Street, one of Motherwell's

The Rex cinema, Motherwell, as it looked in the 1950s.

main thoroughfares and the location of the Rex. The picture house was no more than a minute's walk from our flat.

When I had come in from work on this particular day, Margaret had told me over dinner that a man introducing himself as the manager of the Rex had been at our door earlier, looking to speak with me. Margaret asked if she could take a message and the gentleman told her there had been some strange occurrences in the cinema. He was concerned they might have a ghost. He had been informed of my work, so he wondered if I might be able to look over the cinema for a sign of anything untoward.

A well-groomed, suited man, tall and slender and in his early thirties, came towards me. He asked if I was Tom and I confirmed yes. I shook his outstretched hand as he introduced himself as the cinema's manager. He thanked me for coming in and quickly began telling me what was causing him and his staff concern.

'Mr Robertson, we have cleaners who come in at night and give the auditorium a thorough going over. They go along each row cleaning the floor under the seats, but something odd has been happening as they've been doing this.' He paused.

'And what's that?' I asked.

'Well, the seats are always in an upright position as the cleaners work their way through the rows but as they pass by them, the seats have been coming down and staying down, as if someone is sitting on them. At first, the women thought some of the cinema staff or some kids were hiding in the row behind, pushing the seat in front down with their feet or hands. But after rushing over to catch them in the act and probing the area under the seats with their mops, they realised nothing was there.

'That's not all,' he continued. 'Some of our usherettes have heard unexplained banging in the empty hall and one even saw a figure at the other end of the auditorium that disappeared before her eyes. But nothing seems to happen while the patrons are in the cinema, strangely enough.

'It's been talked about since I started in here, which was

a wee while ago now, and from what I've been told it's been going on for a long time. I've noticed some odd things myself, to be honest. Items have been disappearing from my office: my favourite pen vanished, a logbook, some promotional pieces that had been sent through for new films . . . Some of it hasn't turned up again, others – like my pen – I've found elsewhere in the cinema. I'm convinced I didn't move them. I'm not absent-minded. I wondered if it could have anything to do with what the cleaners and usherettes have been experiencing. I wasn't sure what to do about it, until I heard about yourself.'

'I think you'd better let me have a look around. Are we okay to go into the hall just now?' I asked, walking towards the swing doors to the auditorium. The stream of customers leaving the screening had dried up and the manager said now would be a suitable time as a film had just finished.

I was aware this could just be a publicity attempt and vowed to be extra diligent. But should I discover there really was a haunting in the cinema, I had a nagging feeling it might be exploited to boost business. At a time when just about every town in Scotland had multiple picture houses, the claim of having a resident ghost would make the Rex stand out from the rest.

We pushed through the doors and entered the vast room with its rows and rows of padded, cushioned seats. The huge screen was blank and the lights were up, allowing me to see clearly all around the room. I walked slowly down the aisle, making a cursory glance along each of the rows. I stopped and pulled down on a seat. It came down but when I removed my hand, the cushion flipped back to its original position. The seats were spring-loaded. There was little chance of several seats coming down of their own accord one after the other.

I walked further down the aisle and turned towards the rear of the room in order to have a clear look at the circle upstairs.

The hairs on the back of my neck were standing on end and I felt an unnerving sensation in my gut. There was something here, right enough, so I decided to keep my cards close to my chest for the moment and not express my concerns over the manager's intentions. A presence lurked in this building and by just rolling along and saying nothing untoward at this stage, I knew I would be guaranteed an all-access pass to roam the building.

'Can you take me upstairs?' I asked, pointing to the circle. He nodded and ushered me to follow him. As we walked, I asked what he knew of the history of the building and if anything had happened here that would explain the presence of a ghost.

'Well, there was supposed to have been a suicide here. I'm not sure when or who it was, just that a man jumped from the balcony to the stalls below and died from the fall.'

'That would do it,' I replied. I learned later there was confusion over the location of the supposed suicide. It actually took place in the nearby Old Music Hall, where a middle-aged man stood up in the gallery and slit his throat, dying immediately. However, the death referred to by the Rex's manager occurred when a man fell from the balcony and was killed, back when the venue (the Rex) was known by another name.

The site of the Rex cinema had been one of Motherwell's premier locations for entertainment since shortly after the turn of the twentieth century. Work began on The New Century Theatre in 1901 and the 1,500 capacity variety hall opened the following year. Its architect was Alexander Cullen, along with his newly appointed partners, James Lochhead and William Brown. Cullen was born in nearby Craigneuk, Wishaw, in June 1856 and had worked hard to earn a reputation that resulted in a successful practice. Around the time of the New Century Theatre build, the well-read and intelligent Cullen had offices in Hamilton and Motherwell, and soon after in Glasgow. He was a much in-demand architect.

Cinema historians believe the New Century flirted with the notion of being a cinema shortly before the First World War, when it was renamed the Motherwell Theatre. But in 1915, it reverted back to its original name. At some point in the next few years its name changed once more, this time to the New Century Picture House.

It was sold to the Scottish Cinema and Variety Theatre chain in November 1929 and shortly thereafter the renowned cinema architect Albert Victor Gardner was employed to carry out alterations. Born in Gloucestershire but raised in Glasgow, where he studied at the School of Art, Gardner was renowned as a specialist in cinema architecture, especially for inexpensively built picture houses that were considerably rich and interesting in design. The list of cinemas he was involved with throughout West Central Scotland, whether as a designer or being in charge of reconstruction or alterations, is remarkable. At least one of his cinemas, The Grosvenor in Ashton Lane, the popular upmarket social area in Glasgow's West End, is still operational today.

However, Gardner's alterations weren't to last long. The New Century was closed in 1933 and rebuilding work began. Another architect famous for his cinemas, Ayrshire's Charles James McNair, was in charge of the process. Apart from the façade, very little of the original building remained. It reopened as the Rex cinema on 17 August 1936 with an increased seating capacity of 2,031.

As we talked, the manager and I walked slowly up the stairs and I studied my surroundings. He stood at the back of the circle as I ambled through the rows of seats, stopping to look over the balcony, and gazed down at the stalls below. Aye, that would be enough of a drop to kill a man, if he landed in a particularly nasty fashion. I glanced around and felt a shudder go through me. The cinema could be a spooky place when empty. I returned to my host and he guided me through the various other rooms in the building: the projection room, his office, the staff room and various storage spaces.

A room up in the loft area of the building enticed me. It was located at the front of the cinema, overlooking the distinctive, vertical neon 'REX' sign on the building's façade. The manager unlocked the door and flicked the light switch. It was, as he had told me going in, no more than a storage room and the size of an average home's living room. It was a dusty, cluttered space full of old promotional items like advertising placards and billboard posters for previously screened films.

I walked in and stepped over a discarded forthcoming release notice on the floor and moved as best I could round the limited space. I looked out one of the grimy and dirty windows that remained, past the bright neon sign to the busy street below. This part of the room was an odd shape, almost like an alcove. The front wall was curved and from the outside, visible from the road, it had an odd shape of five angled sections, each with a small window, although two or three of those were boarded up.

The feeling was strong in this room. I removed the coat I

had slung over my forearm and looked at the hairs standing upright. I could feel them prickling against the inside of my shirt further up my arms. I told the manager he definitely had a permanent resident in his cinema and asked how he would like me to proceed. It was late and I didn't plan on starting anything tonight, so it would need to be another occasion. He said he would certainly be in touch and thanked me profusely for my time. He walked me down the flights of stairs and to the front door, where he shook my hand. I stepped out into the cold night, not bothering to pull on my coat for the brief journey home.

Around a week or so later, the manager contacted me again and told me of his imminent plans for the cinema. He was bringing a new film to the Rex called *Pit and the Pendulum*, a horror movie starring Vincent Price based on a short story by Edgar Allan Poe. The tag line on the promotional posters read, 'The greatest Terror Tale ever told!' and the Rex planned to exploit this claim by running a competition in the local press to drum up interest among cinema-goers. They wanted to find a female willing to sit alone in the cinema, who would try to watch the movie from beginning to end without running out. There was no prize to speak of should she successfully endure the entirety of the film but the manager was sure there would be plenty of women wishing to volunteer.

The contest was to be run through the pages of the *Motherwell Times*, which, it transpired, had also been made aware of my confirmation that there was a presence in the cinema. Talks had obviously taken place between the press and the cinema in the interim, and the paper had decided to run an article, not only on how long the competition winner could watch the film but also on the presence haunting the Rex.

What the manager wanted was for me to host a vigil in the cinema in the presence of the journalists to see if Oscar, as the ghost had been dubbed, would show itself. He also requested me to sit in on the screening of *Pit and the Pendulum*, since the lassie would be in there on her own and maybe susceptible to a visit from the shy ghost.

I hesitated. I wasn't too sure about any of this. I wasn't afraid of exposure when it came to my investigations but I had a strong suspicion this entire event may just have been a publicity stunt for the cinema and its new horror film. There was a presence in the cinema; I had no doubt about that. But it was the timing of it all that made me wonder if it was wise to have any part in the proceedings.

Eventually I agreed, since I believed the so-called ghosthunt would go ahead with or without me, and I felt it was better if I had some degree of control over the situation.

The night quickly came around and proceedings began once the usual attractions in the picture house had ended. A young lady who would be celebrating her eighteenth birthday by the time the screening ended at 1 a.m. had been picked from the many entries and, upon entering the cinema, she was presented with a bell. Should the film at any time become too much, she was to ring the bell and the screening would be stopped immediately. She sat near the front of the hall and soon the image of Vincent Price chewing up the scenery filled the big screen. I slipped into the back row to watch over the proceedings while the movie played. Directed by influential B-movie director Roger Corman and featuring a script by horror story maestro Richard Matheson, the film only genuinely chilled in a spine-tingling climax. The female volunteer managed to endure the ninety minutes without ringing the bell and after the credits rolled she was interviewed and photographed by the waiting local press. It probably wasn't the result the cinema manager had hoped for. There were three journalists and photographers, all young, fresh-faced cub reporters probably not long in the door at their newspaper; two men and a female. Too much time has passed for me to remember their names, so let's just call them Ian, Jim and Laura.

Once they had finished with the hardy movie-goer it was my turn. I had requested the vigil take place in the storage room overlooking the Rex sign. Not only had I experienced a strong feeling in there when I was first shown round, but it was also a small, enclosed space. This was important because I could be in control of the situation and not have to worry about any unwanted human interference. I wanted to be aware of any funny tricks going on that might be an attempt to pull the wool over not only my eyes, which would have proved difficult, but also those of the reporters, who might be more susceptible, especially if it meant a juicy story.

The manager led us up the stairs. The three reporters made up the rear and were a few steps behind, walking somewhat tentatively. We gathered in a group at the storage room's heavy wooden door.

'You'll make sure no one comes near this door while we're in here?' I asked the manager.

'Aye, I'll personally make sure of it.'

He brought a key from his pocket and put it in the lock. He turned it and pushed the door open, then pressed down on the light switch. I held the door open for the three reporters, who passed me looking pale and nervous. As I had requested, the room was free of the clutter that had dominated the space when I was last there. There were still a few odds and ends lying against the dusty skirting boards and dark painted walls but there was space to move now . . . and nowhere to hide.

'I'll take that,' I said, motioning towards the key in the manager's hand. 'Is this the only one you have for this door?'

'It is. Are you going to lock it from your side?'

'Yes, sir. We'll be secure in here and I'll unlock it when we're ready to come out.' I stepped into the room and motioned for him to close the door behind me.

'Look, be careful. If you're in any trouble or need . . . I don't know . . . assistance, then just shout or bang on the door. We'll knock it down if you tell us it's an emergency.'

'Right you are,' I said, as I firmly closed the door. I placed the key in the lock, turned it, and pulled on the handle to ensure it was locked. I removed the key and placed it in my trouser pocket. I turned round to be met by three frightened, unsure faces lined up across the room. Behind them were four empty chairs, with a tubular metal frame and curved plywood seat and backrest. They were sturdy but not the most comfortable.

'Jim, Ian, Laura, relax,' I said, walking towards them. 'You know, just because there's a presence in the Rex doesn't mean it will show itself to us tonight. I've been involved in plenty of vigils and ghosthunts and left empty-handed, even though I knew there was something there.' I think they were more expectant than I was of seeing something.

I arranged the seats in a semi-circle in the middle of the floor, with the backs of the chairs pointed towards the windows. I draped my coat over a seat but not before taking a roll of masking tape from one of the pockets. I went over to the remaining windows and began applying large strips of the tape across the panes of glass, making sure to cover the seals as well as blocking out the light from the street. I cut each piece with my teeth until all I could taste was plastic.

I could feel the three sets of eyes boring down on my back and whispered words being exchanged. When I turned round the reporters were looking at me in bewilderment. I walked by the chairs, not saying a word, and applied a long strip of tape down the side of the door. I dropped the remainder of the roll on the floor and stood with my hand on the light switch.

'It's important we do this in complete darkness,' I explained. 'It's also imperative that should anything happen tonight, I know for certain that no human entered this room. The tape across the seals of the windows and the door will ensure I know whether or not that has happened. Now, is everyone happy for the light to be switched off?'

A few uncertain nods of the head were good enough for me as I plunged the room into darkness. I reached into my back pocket and pulled out a torch that I switched on to guide me to my seat. As I sat down I turned it off and placed it face down between my feet. The two men were to my left and Laura to my right. I shifted in the seat as it scraped against the bare wooden floor. I looked around the room, waiting for my eyes to adjust to the pitch darkness.

There were a few coughs and clearing of throats but not much talk and I realised it could be a painfully long evening were I unable to help the reporters loosen up a little. I struck up a quiet-voiced conversation, the details of which were no doubt instantly forgettable, as I tried to pass the time. Never once did I let my guard slip though, as I continued to canvas the room and listen for any unexplainable sounds.

The minutes passed. If I felt nothing was going to happen I was prepared to call it a night early. There was no point in wasting everyone's time. But after a while that feeling was there within me and it grew stronger. The presence was near and I started to believe the journalists might just have something to write about tomorrow.

Those familiar words passed through my mind; 'When I'm about, strange things happen.' As our partnership grew, McGregor and I would be invited to join paranormal groups and research teams. McGregor would always leave the decision to me, but he warned they only wanted me as bait because when I was around whatever presence was there would likely show itself.

And so it was.

'Now, should your nerves get the better of you if something happens, grip your hands tight on the sides of the chair and squeeze. It'll help alleviate some of the tension,' I told them.

'Why? Is something happening?' Laura asked, the nerves clearly audible in her voice.

'I definitely feel it,' I replied. 'Let's just wait and see.' And so we did. More time passed, although it was hard to indicate just how long as we sat in the dark.

Then it started.

A small crack of light appeared in the upper corner of the room, above the door. It was no more than a dot but in the blackness it was like a shining star in the night sky. It was immediately noticeable to all of us. Our eyes fixed on the bright, white light.

It moved ever so slowly towards us . . . agonisingly so. But as it moved it also grew in size and it began to take on a shape. There were squeals either side of me.

'Don't move,' I warned. 'Stay seated.'

The blindingly bright light was almost above our heads when I realised what it was. A human skull. Not a flat, 2-D projection but a fully formed image of a human head. My jaw dropped. This was a new one on me. I heard the chairs around me squeak and shift on the floor as the reporters moved uneasily and gripped as if their lives depended on it. My heart thumped against my chest and I tried to suppress the lump that had formed in my craw.

As the glowing skull floated towards the front of the room, I picked up the torch from between my feet and pointed it in the direction of the head. As the beam shone over it, the skull disappeared.

I couldn't believe what I was seeing.

I turned the torch off with my thumb and the skull re-appeared. I flicked the switch again and the skull was gone just as quickly. I moved the beam up and down the area above and under which the skull had floated, looking for a wire or even someone in black fatigues, and as I did so the skull became visible once more. There were no wires, no poles, no humans . . . just a floating, illuminated, human head.

I turned the torch off but gripped it in my hands as the skull moved back towards us. It passed overhead and glided to its starting position, shrinking in size and losing its clarity and shape. By the time it was in the corner above the door it was again no more than a piercingly bright dot. And then it was gone. Its journey couldn't have lasted any more than a minute.

I jumped up and rushed towards that corner, flicking on the light switch to my right hand side. I blinked for the first time since the skull had appeared. All I could see when I closed my eyes was its bright outline.

I looked up to the corner from where it had appeared and promptly disappeared. The wall was completely solid, not even a crack in the plaster. I knocked my fist against the concrete several times at different heights but it was rock-hard. These were thick stone walls in which we were encased.

I turned to my left and ran my fingers down the door. The tape was still firmly in place. I looked over to the windows and could see they, too, were undisturbed. My attention shifted to Ian, Jim and Laura. Their faces were almost as white as the skull that had just passed over them. They sat so rigid I could have sworn rigor mortis had set in. They had been so shocked that the photographer hadn't even reached for his camera.

'Well, it's safe to say that was your first experience of a ghost,' I announced, catching my breath. My heart continued to race. 'I think it's time we got you out of here.' I reached into my pocket and brought out the key and turned it in the lock, pulling open the door. Jim and Ian were so close I could feel their breath on the back of my neck. I stepped aside and let them rush by. I looked round and saw Laura was standing in the centre of the room. She looked terrified.

'It's okay, Laura. You can leave now.' I hoped I said it in a reassuring manner.

She nodded in response.

'Right. Well, you'd better let go of that chair if you're planning on going.'

Although standing upright, the poor lassie still had a vice-like grip on the chair, which she grasped behind her in the clutches of her white-knuckled hands. She didn't even realise until I pointed it out. She placed the chair down on the floor and pulled her hair back from her face as she walked out of the room.

'Are you all right?' I asked as she walked past.

'I think so,' she said meekly, making a cursory glance towards me as she stared at the ground.

I followed her out of the room, where an exasperated-looking manager met us. He wanted to know what had happened, so

I filled him in. The three reporters allowed me to do most of the talking; I think they were struggling to comprehend what they had witnessed. The harassed manager seemed genuinely surprised when I told him but he didn't appear to be frightened or concerned. If anything he seemed quite glad to hear the news.

I asked how he wanted to proceed from here, although since it had been a long and tiring night for everyone involved whatever plans he had might be best put on hiatus, overnight at least. He agreed and asked if I would mind popping by the cinema tomorrow. Ian, Jim and Laura took a few minutes to sort themselves out and gather their belongings, before the manager walked us down the flights of stairs to the front door.

I shook hands with the reporters as we stepped out into the cold wind that breezed along Windmillhill Street and asked them to please write an accurate report that reflected what we had encountered. The cold air must have reawakened their senses because I left them huddled in the doorway, their tongues now wagging furiously. They might only have been novice reporters setting out on the first steps of their journalistic journeys, but I was willing to bet should their careers last forty more years they would never have another assignment like this one.

As I walked round the corner to my home, I couldn't shake the image of the brightly lit skull hovering through the air. It didn't help, of course, that every time I closed my eyes the intense light flashed in front of me.

After a broken night's sleep I returned to the Rex and met with the manager. I thought he might ask me to rid his premises of Oscar, as he continually called the presence. He did not. Instead, he went into his pocket and brought out a card. 'I'd

like you to have this as a thank you for all your time and effort,'
he said. 'It's been greatly appreciated. This is a free pass to
get into any and all screenings at the Rex. You'll never have
to pay to watch another film here again.'

I thanked him and said it was a kind gesture, but what did
he intend to do about 'Oscar'? He replied that he was comfortable in the knowledge that the cinema did indeed have a
ghost, one that seemed to delight in causing mischief and
frights rather than attempting to hurt anyone.

This conversation confirmed my earlier suspicions. It
seemed to me he wanted to use the ghost as a publicity stunt,
probably to boost the fear factor among patrons who queued
up to watch the latest horror release. Although the manager
and staff said Oscar had been calling the Rex home for a
number of years and had never brought harm to anyone, I
still thought it was a risky move. As I left the cinema it seemed
to me his scheme was a gamble that could go one of two ways.
The picture house would either receive a boost from the press
and those patrons who were keen to watch a spooky film in
a haunted cinema, or it would lead to a fall in customers for
the opposite reason.

As for me, I returned to the Rex cinema that same week. I
did have a free pass, after all, and it was no more than a stone's
throw from my home. So I went twice in the first week. When
I returned a third time, the woman at the ticket booth told
me under instruction from her manager I had to hand in the
card. I was no longer permitted to use it. I asked her what
was wrong and she replied, 'You've already used it twice this
week. That's it finished with. No more.' She opened a drawer
and threw the card inside. I couldn't believe it! Talk about
gratitude.

So, that was the end of the Rex for me. However, Oscar

did do me a good turn. The press cuttings from the local newspaper about our special night at the movies had come to the attention of researchers at the BBC's *Tonight* team. My job intrigued them and the end result was the first attempt at a televised exorcism, on The Black Lady of Broomhill House in Larkhall. As for the newspaper report from Jim, Ian and Laura in the *Motherwell Times*, I was happy to see them tell the story just as it happened.

I was never able to explain what I saw that night, although I knew it wasn't faked. Even McGregor, when I told him, said it was a new one on him.

As it transpired, Oscar did receive plenty of publicity and the story of the cinema ghost became a well-told tale in the area. Even today, the story remains familiar to the locals and it didn't seem to harm the cinema's box office too much, at least for a while. The Rex continued to plough on through the years, entertaining the customers with the latest big titles from Hollywood and the possibility of an appearance from Oscar itself.

The cinema closed its doors for the last time in June 1976, although the building continued to live on as a place of entertainment, firstly as an amusement complex and later as a snooker hall and nightclub. I wasn't aware of any noted sightings or disturbances from Oscar during this period. Perhaps his love was for the cinema and when the screen faded to black for the final time he decided there would be no more cameos.

The façade of the building changed dramatically when the Rex closed. The famous vertical sign and the 'coming attractions' bill along the top of the entrance were boxed in to make way for a considerably blander frontage. Above it, though, the room in the upper floor remained and, over the years, each time I passed by the old Rex I looked up at the storage loft's windows and recalled that astounding night at the pictures in the 1960s.

The curtain came down on the old building when it was demolished in the spring of 1995. Oscar would certainly have gone then. But I will never forget the performance he put on that night or the role he played in my own blossoming career.

5

Tower of Sighs

As usual, McGregor greeted us politely and graciously as he pulled open the heavy door of the grand old house and motioned us inside. Willie and I came in from the early evening sunlight and walked towards our mentor's office. It was our headquarters so to speak, the place where we discussed all of our business affairs. Many a weird and wonderful adventure had been planned and plotted within those book-laden walls. The yellowing pages of those dusty old books, telling tales that could never measure up to our own fantastic chronicles, were sole witness to many private and clandestine conversations that could never leave that room, our words floating up to the high ceiling and dispersing like the smoke that billowed from McGregor's pipe.

We sat around the rectangular wooden table and watched as he picked up a letter and passed it to me. This was nothing unusual. In fact, it was strange if even a short passage of time went by without someone coming to us for help.

It was 1968, and thankfully the constant stream of letters and phone calls pleading for assistance that had beset us for such a long time had reduced to a steady filter. When I went public in Scotland with what I did, I knew I was providing a service for so many people who had encountered something otherworldly but did not know where to turn. Before me, the affected would desperately seek help from the local priest or minister, not knowing what else to do. I wanted those who were experiencing paranormal happenings to know they weren't crazy and there was someone who could help. I brought an unspoken and somewhat embarrassing issue into the mainstream and became the conduit between these people and the spirit that haunted them.

And boy, did people respond.

It was as if I'd picked the lock to Hell's post office, as correspondence describing all sorts of monstrosities and frightening encounters piled up around us.

Of course, there were plenty of disbelievers and agenda-driven individuals that would try to expose or humiliate both my work and myself. The appearance I made on an early episode of one of Scottish Television's first shows, *Late Night Final*, is a good example of what I often faced. Willie accompanied me as I drove to Glasgow in my Armstrong Coupé to the STV studios, which were located in the Theatre Royal in the city centre. STV had gone on air in August 1957 and used the old theatre as its studios for the first fourteen years, recording most of the station's output on the stage.

I was to be interviewed by a presenter called Douglas Keay, who took a rather condescending demeanour and tone with me. When it was my turn to go on camera I was led out to the stage and he sat down opposite. From the outset of the interview his remit was clear. He told me he didn't believe in ghosts and asked why I expected others to believe what I told them about the supernatural. As far as I was concerned he was as much as accusing me of being a fraud. The chat continued in this vein for a few moments until I decided enough was enough.

When I had been introduced to Keay earlier, I noticed through the top of his open-neck shirt a cross round his neck.

'Do you believe in God?' I asked him, interrupting his flow of questions. Obviously perturbed by the direct line of inquiry, he nevertheless answered and said he did.

'Do you believe in Jesus Christ?' I continued. Yes.

'And do you believe He came back from the dead?' Yes.

'Well, you believe in the biggest ghost of them all, don't you?'

His tone changed for the rest of the interview and he displayed a little more humility. He obviously hadn't been expecting me to turn the tables but I was always ready for frauds or disbelievers. I could tell when someone was on the make. My eyes were like an eagle's and I had a photographic memory in those days. I don't know what happened in subsequent years; maybe the switchover to digital fried my brain!

Back in the early days, our team had never been backwards at giving out our contact details, usually McGregor's, and almost every national newspaper had our information on file, so we were easily reachable. We helped a lot of people. Many of them asked for confidentiality and that is an agreement I have never broken, even decades on.

But at one stage I couldn't handle it all. Willie wanted no part of the media attention and only occasionally would McGregor make his voice heard, so I was the poster boy and go-to man for anything deemed supernatural. It was engulfing me and taking over my life. I still had a full-time job to concentrate on and a wife and children, but I could barely make it through a week without being stopped in the street or contacted by someone frantic with worry about matters they couldn't comprehend.

I read the letter and handed it to Willie.

'Can you boys make it tomorrow night?' McGregor asked.

I told him I could and Willie stopped reading and looked up from the letter to nod his head in the affirmative.

The letter was fairly brief and to the point. It was from Kinneil Estate, a historically important but little known place near Bo'ness in Falkirk. The workers there had recently encountered a strange disturbance in the old tower house attached to the grand home. They could only describe it as a very loud sighing or heavy breathing, as booming as a giant with a megaphone. The noise would reverberate and drift up the bare brick walls of the tower causing alarm to the staff, especially the caretaker, who was finding his job rather uncomfortable all of a sudden. We had been recommended to them and the letter asked if we might find it possible to make our way through at our earliest convenience.

Between reading the letter and travelling to Bo'ness the following evening, McGregor filled us in on the history of a place I knew very little about.

Kinneil was an ancient village and parish not too far from the River Forth. Today, only scarce remnants linger as a reminder of what once was; a one-mile area containing artefacts covering 2,000 years of Scottish history.

The Antonine Wall, the northern boundary of the Roman Empire, once cut across the area that would become known as Kinneil. Although very few traces of the wall remains today (a stone base built up with turf and dirt), the markings of a Roman fort are still visible. A short distance from that are the remnants of Kinneil Church, believed to have been built originally in the 1100s. The distinct double belfry attached to an outer wall, along with a smattering of grave slabs, are all that is left of the church that formed the centre point of Kinneil village by the fifteenth century.

In the 1400s, a small tower house was built on land in front of the church. The land had been gifted by Robert I to Walter Fitzgilbert of Hamilton, the family that later produced the Dukes of Hamilton, and Kinneil became their base when they were in the East. It was the prominent and powerful Hamilton dynasty that built the tower, which overlooked a deep ravine carved out by the Gil Burn. The tower was enlarged in the late 1400s or early 1500s and a palace was erected a short distance from the tower in 1553, which boasted extensive views of the countryside and the Firth of Forth. An expansion

It was in this main part of Kinneil House, near Bo'ness, that a strange noise emanated which had all of Scotland talking and prompted staff to contact Tom and McGregor.

of Kinneil House in 1667 saw the tower and palace become attached.

It was during that redevelopment and expansion that the villagers belonging to Kinneil were uprooted and moved to the growing town of Bo'ness, and the village effectively died away.

Around a century later, the Hamiltons stopped using Kinneil House and it was rented out to a number of tenants. Among them was Doctor John Roebuck, the owner of the first ironworks in Scotland, at Carron. Roebuck's enterprise led him to coal mining, where he hoped to secure a supply of fuel for the ironworks. He took over the lease of the Duke of Hamilton's coalmines at Boroughstoness and Kinneil House came as part of the deal, so he moved into the tranquil home.

When Roebuck began sinking for coal, he realised the engine he was using to keep the mines clear of water was insufficient for its purpose. He was put in touch with a young man called James Watt, who was working on a new, more powerful steam engine. Roebuck gave Watt the use of an outhouse at the rear of Kinneil House where he could work on his experiments and, while he did make improvements, it wasn't until after his time at Kinneil had concluded that he came up with a steam engine capable of pumping the water out of the mines.

The last tenant of the house was the philosopher, Dugald Stewart, who proposed many of his theories there between 1809 and 1828.

In 1922, Bo'ness Town Council bought over the estate and, in 1936, work started to demolish Kinneil House. They began in the tower house, which had its interiors completely gutted, leaving only the bare walls.

When the workers moved onto the house, they happened

upon magnificent wall and ceiling paintings that were remarkably well preserved. Located mainly in the Arbour and Parable rooms, they are believed to date from the sixteenth and seventeenth centuries. The discovery halted the planned demolition and Kinneil Estate thankfully lived on.

All that is missing from such a colourful and wonderful history is a resident ghost story. Well, read on.

The tale goes that Oliver Cromwell sent an officer called General Lilbourne, or Lilyburn, to Scotland in 1651 and Kinneil House was to be his base. Lilbourne had only just married and didn't want to leave his new bride, Lady Alice, behind, so she accompanied him on his travels. Apparently, she quickly became homesick and pleaded for a return to England, which led to many arguments and an unhappy marriage. Upset after one such disagreement, Lilbourne snapped and locked Lady Alice, who wore only a white nightgown, in an attic room overlooking the ravine through which the Gil Burn flows. She escaped but was recaptured and thrown once again into the attic. This time she could take no more and, seeing no way out of her miserable predicament, she jumped to her death from the attic window to the rocks on the ravine almost 200 feet below.

Another version of the story, popular in local circles, is that she threw herself into the ravine after she and her lover were caught trying to elope. Local legend claims he was entombed alive in a hollow tree.

Lady Alice, or the White Lady as she became known thanks to her attire at the time of her death, became a familiar tale in the area and the stories were passed down from generation to generation.

On Kinneil's website there is a reprint of a letter from nineteenth-century writer Maria Edgeworth, who tells of her

It was from the rear of this tower block that a young woman is said to have fallen to her death into the Gil Burn directly below.

stay in the house and makes mention of the ghost. Dated 2 June 1823, the extract reads:

> Mrs Stewart told us this morning that there were plenty of ghosts at our service belonging to Kinneil House. One, in particular, Lady Lilyburn, who is often seen all in white, as a ghost should be, and with white wings, fluttering on top of the castle, from whence she leaps into the sea – a prodigious leap of three or four hundred yards, nothing for a well-bred ghost. At other times she wears boots, and stumps up and down stairs in them, and across passages, and through bedchambers, frightening ladies' maids and others. We have not heard her . . . yet.

McGregor, Willie and I knew the reports of the noises from the tower house would, inevitably, be linked to the White Lady, but we were long enough in the tooth not to jump to conclusions. We would carry out our own investigations without prejudice.

As we drove through the freestanding stone gateposts and moved slowly along the drive towards the impressive and daunting house, we noticed a horde of people standing around the exterior of the building. Obviously word had spread in the area about the noises and an expectant crowd congregated, perhaps hoping for a glimpse of poor Lady Alice, three centuries after her demise.

We parked the car and collected our equipment from the boot. We always went to jobs well prepared and ready to cover all bases and eventualities. As the nineteenth-century English writer and cleric, Charles Caleb Colton, said: 'Examinations are formidable even to the most prepared, for the greatest fool may ask more than the wisest man can answer.' No matter the situation and location, whether it was to investigate a haunting or expose a fraud, we would turn up ready and equipped.

McGregor had one of the first portable reel-to-reel tape recorders. It was small for the time but looking back it was big, heavy and cumbersome. It came in a sturdy leather case and was around a foot long and six inches deep, with a number of cables running from it. However, it was an effective machine and McGregor would record many of our investigations to pick up any strange noises, not only for posterity but also for further examination when we were away from the scene.

Willie picked up his super-sensitive metal detector. He had built it from scratch from old parts he had collected here and there. It had huge headphones that he wore to listen for any underground discrepancies. A cloth-covered chord, like the cable on a telephone receiver, stretched from the headphones to the machinery and another cable for the rechargeable battery pack also ran from the detector.

Willie brought it on jobs to check for anything unusual under floors and ground that might be causing movement or noises. Even a disused pipe under the earth could be the cause of strange sounds and provide the solution to the 'ghost' that had been haunting a property. On more than one occasion, we had checked an area for buried treasure that had supposedly been hidden; not a wooden chest full of gold coins, of course, but valuables that were said to have been secreted years before. We never did locate any treasure but, even if we had, I wouldn't be disclosing it now!

I was wearing the camera Willie had made from a wristwatch. I had taken to wearing it to most of our investigations, even when McGregor brought his own camera. But I tended to rely on my instincts and the gifts I had been blessed with . . . or cursed with, depending on whom you asked. We each had our individual strengths and mine didn't require any cutting edge technology.

We all carried heavy-duty torches. It would soon be dark and obviously the tower had no electricity, so these were essential. Willie had tampered with them to make them even brighter, replacing the bulbs with his own. The batteries didn't last so long but it gave the torches maximum exposure.

As we walked towards the group of intrigued locals waiting eagerly for the sounds that had left the staff at Kinneil spooked, a camera flash caught our attention. We looked off to the right of the crowd and saw two men, one of whom had a camera hanging around his neck, standing against the wall of the house. They waved as we acknowledged them and came to meet us.

When McGregor had called Kinneil House earlier that day to accept the invitation and to tell them we would be through in the evening, he was asked if we would mind a newspaper reporter and photographer coming along to document the investigation. We had often worked with the media during live enquiries so McGregor said it was fine, so long as they kept a distance and didn't interfere in any way. It also alerted us to the possibility that this was nothing more than a publicity stunt.

We introduced ourselves and made some small talk, just as a gentleman came out of the house and approached us. He was the caretaker and he asked all five of us to come inside until the crowd dispersed. He said the throng had been growing steadily over the past few days after word had spread about the noises, but they didn't tend to wait into the night.

'They're nosey and keen, but not enough to stand about in the dark with their bellies rumbling,' he laughed. But his

Beyond this padlocked, reinforced steel doorway, Tom, McGregor and Willie were to uncover the truth behind the strange noises attributed to the supposed ghost of Kinneil House.

easy-going tone was markedly absent when we began asking questions about those sounds. It was obvious from his demeanour and the nervousness in his voice that whatever he had heard had genuinely disturbed him.

It came no more than once a day but could last for a long time when it did arrive. It was loud, not deafening, but noisy all the same. It was hearing breathing at that volume, bouncing from wall to wall inside the tower, which left him shaken.

As we talked, he guided us round the impressive building, passing through the rooms with the beautiful paintings. After a while he glanced out one of the windows and, seeing that the crowd had dispersed, guided us downstairs and towards the tower house.

He unlocked the door and led us in. The first thing I did once inside was bend down and tuck my trousers into my socks. I saw the pressmen staring at me.

'Rats,' I said, as I stood up and looked around.

Once upon a time there would have been several floors within the tower but these had been removed. I stretched my head back to look up at the plain stone walls, all the way to the top.

In one corner of the floor were the remnants of a staircase; just a dozen or so steps had survived the deconstruction. I walked over to them and saw there was a large pile of straw under the stairs. A handful of raw potatoes and an old billycan rested on top and I wondered if a tramp had been squatting here, although the door had been locked when the caretaker brought us round. If it was a vagrant, maybe he had also heard the strange noise and left these belongings behind when he fled in fear.

There wasn't much we could check in the sparse surroundings but we did what we could and then we waited. Time passed, maybe an hour or so, with the sound of the wind and the bristling trees outside the only accompaniment to our quiet, sporadic conversation. Willie, McGregor and I were prepared to wait through the night if need be, but even then there were no guarantees we would be privy to the mystery of the heavy breathing.

I was sitting with my back against the wall when I first heard the different noise. At first, I thought the wind was picking up but on closer listening I noted it was still blowing as gently as before. There was another noise and this was coming from inside the tower.

I looked at McGregor, who returned my glance, and then to Willie, who I could see was staring back at us, nodding his head in unspoken understanding. As I stood I watched McGregor pick up the tape recorder and press down on the play and record buttons. He held the battery-sized microphone in his outstretched left hand.

Hush, hush, hush.

It was a steady, controlled and repetitive noise. It began as nothing more than a whisper but with each successive *hush* the sound grew louder, until it reached such a crescendo that it really could have been the breathing pattern of a giant.

The reporter and photographer stood agape as the caretaker looked on knowingly. I have to admit to being taken aback. I think all three of us were surprised. Often the personal accounts of a case are overexaggerated and I choose to remain impartial until I investigate a disturbance, but everything we had been told about the invisible presence's heavy breathing was true.

The three of us congregated in the centre of the floor, and Willie and I flashed our torches over the walls.

'It might be a recording,' McGregor said firmly but quietly, making sure no one outside our circle could hear. He continued to clutch his own recorder in his fisted right hand. 'See those holes in the walls? We need to check them, at least the ones we can reach, to ensure there're no tape recorders or speakers hidden inside.'

The rectangular spaces stretched all the way up the height of the tower. At one time the beams for each floor would have fitted in those holes. Although the walls of the tower appeared to be several feet thick, in actual fact they were made up of two thinner walls separated by a duct running between them. We would only be able to access the first level of holes but if something was hidden there it would hopefully be in one of those spaces, since the higher holes would have been difficult to reach without a ladder.

I walked off to the side, more than a little hesitant of fulfilling McGregor's task. I stood below a hole and shone the torchlight inside but from my angle I couldn't tell if there was anything hidden.

The sound continued to reverberate around us.

I felt the sweat form on my brow and beads of perspiration roll down my spine as I tried to force myself to lift my free hand towards the hole and check inside. I took a deep breath and blinked hard. Lifting my arm slowly, I placed my hand tentatively on the edge of the hole. Quickly, I pushed it all the way in, patting around the empty space before pulling it out in a blur of movement.

I was terrified of rats. I've always had a phobia of the rodents and I was scared I might place my hand on one scurrying around the ducts. It might sound surprising, considering the places I've been and the sights I've witnessed, but I would rather confront a ghost than a rat.

I flashed my torch towards the walls where McGregor and Willie worked and saw them move from hole to hole with speed and thoroughness. I forced myself to check one more hole then surrendered. My partners could inspect the remainder.

Just then, Willie let out a gasp. 'C'mere lads,' he shouted. We rushed over.

'I just touched something in there.' He pointed at the hole above his head. 'It was an animal . . . a bird, I think.'

The noise had stopped.

'Do you hear it?' I asked them. 'It's stopped. Just like that.'

We looked back up at the hole and just then we saw two tiny, beady eyes appear. I shone the torch in their direction. Lady Alice it most definitely was not.

'My God, it's a pigeon,' McGregor remarked.

I hoisted Willie so he could see directly into the hole by the light of the torch.

'There's more in here,' he said. They're cooried down. They've been sleeping.'

'That's what the noise has been,' McGregor realised.

As I eased Willie back down to the ground, the other three men had joined us and stood beside McGregor. There was a visible sign of relief on the caretaker's face.

'Are you saying the pigeons have been making that sound?' the reporter asked McGregor, a disbelieving tone in his voice. 'You heard the racket. There's no way a few pigeons, or even an entire flock, could create that volume.'

'It's just like the mausoleum,' I said.

McGregor and Willie immediately knew what I meant but it was lost on the rest. I was referring to Hamilton Mausoleum; a domed structure over 100 feet high that was built in the mid-nineteenth century, near to the now demolished Hamilton Palace. In fact, it is the only building remaining from the once grandiose Hamilton Low Parks.

Alexander, the tenth Duke of Hamilton, was interred there in an Egyptian sarcophagus in the main chapel, while seventeen of his ancestors were laid to rest in the crypt below, although

The exterior of the imposing Hamilton Mausoleum, which is reputed to have the longest lasting echo in the world, a phenomenon that Tom recalled when investigating the strange noises coming from within Kinneil House.

they were all later removed after subsidence and flooding affected the mausoleum.

Somewhat miraculously, the subsidence settled and the building returned to a near vertical position. Even more amazingly though, are the acoustics within the mausoleum. Not only does it have the longest lasting echo in the world but it also boasts the Whispering Walls, where two people can stand at opposite ends of the building, facing away from each other, and conduct a whispered conversation with perfect clarity.

The sound of the pigeons sleeping and snoring had travelled

round the ducts and built up in volume to create the effect of some huge creature breathing heavily, thanks to the unusual acoustics of the tower house.

It was living proof that the unexplained sometimes could, in fact, be explained by natural means.

'Sorry, boys,' I said to the newspapermen. 'It's no ghost story this time round but it's still a hell of a tale. I look forward to reading it.'

The reporter paused before replying, 'I still can't believe it's only been pigeons. It was so loud.'

'Sometimes the living world is just as strange as the other-worldly,' McGregor countered, as he turned off his tape recorder and headed towards the door. Willie picked up his metal detector and followed him out. We shook hands with the boys from the paper and the caretaker, who thanked us profusely and said he would be checking for holes in the exterior walls of the tower house the next morning, and we made our way back to the car.

The next night I settled down after eating dinner to watch the STV news. They went to a segment by reporter Bill Tennant and, would you believe it, he was on location at Kinneil Estate to report on the loud, mysterious breathing emanating from the tower house.

A group of people continued to mill around outside, hoping to hear the phenomenon. 'They're milking this,' I muttered, as the report played out. The staff could have told STV before Bill Tennant and his gang travelled through that the noise had been explained and it was no ghost, but they were obviously happy to accept the extra publicity. Tennant had a team of so-called psychic investigators with him, who confirmed on camera that there was definitely a spirit nearby, which was the source of the sound. I laughed hard.

I knew the article wouldn't appear in that day's newspaper but I was surprised when it was not in the following day's edition, either. Unbeknownst to me, the reporter had taken time off after his late night field trip, so it was a few days before it finally appeared in print.

Sure enough, the rest of the Scottish media and press picked up on the story, without directly acknowledging the source of the discovery.

They all tried to appear clever after the event, but in reality their tale of ghosts was nothing but a flight of fancy inspired by pigeons with a penchant for snoring.

A spirited sleep, one might say.

6

A Haunting on Merseyside

While it's fair to say that most of my work has been conducted in Scotland during my long career, it certainly was not unusual at one time to find myself crossing the border – and occasionally further afield – to carry out an investigation. Stretching back to the early days with McGregor, I can recall driving down to England to check out a rumoured haunting or to debunk a fraudulent psychic who was exploiting and ripping off the vulnerable. As the years rolled on, I continued to go beyond Hadrian's Wall to help those in need, as news of my specialised line of work became better known.

Margaret and I were living in the historic town of Lanark when I received a letter in the post that would lead to one of my more memorable trips to England.

'There's a letter here for you,' Margaret told me as I came into the kitchen. I lifted the envelopes from the table and leafed through them, expecting to find unwanted bills. Sure enough, there were a couple of official looking letters with my name printed on the front in bold lettering. But in between the usual unwanted dispatches was a small, handwritten brown envelope. I discarded the other mail, sliced along the top of the envelope to open it and pulled out a folded piece of lined paper that had been hastily ripped from a notebook, as indicated by the missing corner of the page.

Judging by the style of the handwriting I was of the mind that the writer was an elderly person, although the note didn't state so much. Once I had finished reading it, I passed it to Margaret to seek her opinion.

Harry lived in Liverpool and had recently read about me in the *Sunday Post,* which, despite being a Scottish newspaper, had a huge readership in England at the time, thanks in part to the patriotic Scots who had moved south and continued to buy the paper. Harry said he had a problem and after reading about me, he thought I might be able to help.

That was it. Nothing more explanatory than 'a problem'.

He listed his address but advised he had no telephone, which didn't make my life any easier.

'What do you think?' I asked Margaret, once she had finished reading.

'I don't know. It doesn't say much, does it? It looks like it was written by an old person, though,' she replied. 'He could just be lonely or he may be going senile. But then again, he might actually be genuinely scared and need some help.'

We continued to discuss it over breakfast and by the time I had swallowed the last of my tea, the decision had been made that I should drive down to see the old fellow.

After confirming with directory inquiries that they had no number for someone of Harry's name at the address given, I decided on the spur of the moment to drive down to Liverpool that very day. It was still fairly early and I didn't have any plans, so it made sense to go as soon as possible to see what I could do for Harry, even if simply to reassure him. It was hard not to be sceptical when I received a letter of this type but the simple fact is that the overwhelming majority of such correspondence, and all investigations in general, prove to have a straightforward explanation. Believe me, ghosts do not just appear the moment I step out of my house.

I gathered myself together and picked up the keys to my Rover, with Harry's letter folded in my pocket and my detailed road map of Great Britain tucked under my arm. I told Margaret I'd call her from a service station or call box when I arrived in Liverpool to let her know I was safe, and with that I climbed into the car and began my long drive.

By mid afternoon, after stopping to ask for directions once or twice, I had located the street noted on Harry's letter.

I drove slowly along the road, peering out the window for any sign of a street number listed on the front of the various buildings; there were shops, houses, a couple of pubs, it was a typical thoroughfare. Eventually I pulled up in front of a large, fairly new looking building that was all on the one level and had a welcoming glass frontage.

I made my way inside. There was a reception just off to the side, where a man dressed in a shirt and tie sat reading a newspaper. I presumed I was in an old folks' home or sheltered housing complex.

I approached the desk and asked the gentleman if he knew if someone by Harry's name lived there. He ran his finger down a list on a sheet that was taped to the desk and gave me a room number, and then directed me to the right. I walked along the brightly lit, carpeted corridor, passing by a series of wood panelled doors, each a self-contained flat. I arrived at the door and pressed the bell. I heard movement from within the flat and the door slowly opened to reveal a well-dressed man who was maybe seventy years old, of average height, slim built with thin white hair.

'Harry?' I asked, clutching his letter in my hand so it was visible.

'Mr Robertson? I only sent you that letter a couple of days ago. I didn't expect to hear from you so soon. I wasn't sure if I'd hear from you at all, truth be told. Please, come in.' The elderly man stood to the side and let me pass, and then closed the door firmly behind me.

'Into the left there, Mr Robertson,' he said in his thick Liverpudlian accent.

I passed an open door that revealed a bedroom with a single bed and some basic furniture. There was a closed door opposite that I presumed was the bathroom before the L-shaped hallway opened out into a modest sized living room with an adjoining kitchen. It was clean and well-kept, but the old-fashioned furniture and trinkets jarred the senses in comparison with the modern building.

Harry told me to take a seat and offered me a cup of tea, which I gladly accepted. As he prepared the drinks in the kitchen I watched him closely. He moved well for his age and seemed to be completely lucid as he made small talk while stirring the milk into his mug.

'I don't believe in ghosts, you know,' he said, as he handed me a cup and sat down in an armchair directly across from me. 'Well, I didn't . . . I still don't. It's just that I have no idea what's going on. I've not been here very long and if I try to tell the warden what's been happening I'm frightened he'll think I'm losing my mind and they'll put me in a home. So when I saw you in the paper and the work you did, I decided to contact them to see if they'd give me your address.'

'Aye, I told the reporter that if anyone contacted him off the back of the article he should pass on my address, so folk like yourself could write to me. Tell me what's been happening, Harry.'

'You'll think I'm mad but every night when I go to my bed there's this strange noise starts right above my head. It sounds like a banging or loud snapping, as if someone is clapping their hands next to my ear. I open my eyes and it stops, I close them and it starts again. At first I thought it was coincidence. Then I thought it was one of the neighbours making a noise. But it went on for God knows how many hours that first night and it's happened nearly every night since. I even thought I was half sleeping and imagining the whole thing, but it's been carrying on for so long now that I know it's real. It's left me exhausted.'

We chatted a little while longer and then I went into his bedroom and had a look around. I'd experienced a slight feeling of a presence the entire time I'd been in Harry's house, but it was so weak that I doubted whatever it was would have the power to make such a noise. The feeling wasn't any stronger in this room. I also considered that this entity could be in a different part of the building, and it may actually have been another elderly resident who was in need of my assistance rather than Harry.

After conducting a thorough search of the place I returned to my seat across from the old man.

'Harry, did you serve during the war?'

'I wasn't in the forces but I was a merchant seaman. I was torpedoed twice.' He shook his head and stared beyond me as he said the words, the statement no doubt flashing images across his mind that were too horrific for most people to even imagine.

I knew all about the merchant seamen, brave men – and

occasionally women – who are often overlooked when history recognises the sacrifices made by the British people in keeping our country out of Hitler's hands.

The Allied Merchant Navy was made up of Britons primarily, alongside men from other countries in the Commonwealth and Allied nations. Even though they were non-military, the merchant seamen faced as many dangers as those in the forces while attempting to carry out their responsibilities. Their mission was to transport vital food, fuel and equipment to wherever it was needed. They did this in vessels not designed or equipped to properly defend against the enemy, which usually came in the form of the U-boat.

From the outset of war, the Merchant Navy found itself under attack, and the unrelenting enemy sent approximately 30,000 British merchant seamen to their watery graves.

The Pom's potato powder and dried egg that I remembered so well from my childhood was brought to these shores from North America by men such as Harry as they struggled to survive the Battle of the Atlantic, recognised by many to be the longest continuous conflict of the Second World War. While our Allies were struggling, it was these supplies that saw Britain cling on during the darker days when Nazi Germany was in the ascendancy.

Much of the Battle of the Atlantic was waged from head-quarters in Liverpool and today there is a memorial to the merchant seamen overlooking the city's shores.

For Harry to have survived being torpedoed once was remarkable; twice was simply amazing. Those seamen who weren't killed instantly from a torpedo attack would often succumb to drowning, hypothermia, a lack of rescue ships or any other number of tragic deaths, so I knew this extraordinary man before me must have endured unthinkable horrors.

'Harry, have you ever suffered from shellshock? You know, it can come on at any time. There's no time limit; no matter how many years may have passed since the incidents, it can just come upon you without warning.'

However, he was not for accepting this theory. Harry was adamant that the late-night banging in his bedroom was real and not a hangover from his war days.

I spent the next couple of hours chatting with him and, over the course of my visit, he seemed to relax and become more at ease. I enjoyed his company and I believe the feeling was mutual, but I was aware of the drive that faced me and I told him I would soon have to go. I was also aware that the strength of the already weak presence had been fading during my time in the house.

I told Harry that should anything else untoward happen or if the banging continued, he must ask to use the warden's telephone to call me. I wrote down my number and told him not to hesitate in contacting me if he needed my help. He walked me to the front door as I set out on the long journey home.

Around two weeks later, I received a call early one morning from Harry's building superintendent. I didn't need to ask if anything was wrong because I could hear the bewilderment in his voice.

'Is Harry okay?' I asked.

'I don't know . . . I think so. He's had a hell of a time of it these past couple of days and things have taken a further turn for the worse. I don't know how to even begin to explain what's happened because I can't understand any of it myself, but we need you down here urgently. Can you make it today?'

'Eh, aye, I can probably be down there by mid-afternoon. Is it bad, whatever it is that's happened?'

'Bad? I would say so. "Mad" is probably a better word, to be honest. But it's best you see it for yourself.'

We said our goodbyes and I hung up the phone and explained the conversation to Margaret. Within ten minutes I was in the car and on my way back to Liverpool.

I made good time and pulled up outside the sheltered housing complex ahead of schedule. Standing at the reception as I rushed through the doors was a middle-aged man, who asked if my name was Tom Robertson. I told him it was and a look of relief flushed over his face as he explained that it was him I had spoken to on the phone that morning. I wondered how long he had been standing there on tenterhooks waiting for me.

'Come with me,' he said in an exasperated tone. I was led round the corner and down the corridor towards Harry's place.

'What's been happening?' I asked, trying to keep up.

'I believe you know all about the strange banging he's been complaining about?'

'Aye, I was down a couple of weeks ago seeing him.'

'Well, it seems he mentioned the problem to one of the other residents a few days ago. It so happens that this resident is very religious and she contacted her priest. He came to see Harry the next day.'

By this time we were outside Harry's door. The superintendent opened it and ushered me in. Harry was standing in the hallway, looking decidedly pensive.

'Are you all right, Harry?' I placed my hand on his stooped shoulder. Even in the dim light of the windowless hall I could see the worry etched on his face.

'Oh Mr Robertson, I don't know. I'm sorry for having to drag you down here again but things have got worse and I'm terrified. I don't know what's happening, to be perfectly honest.'

'This gentleman here was just telling me you had a priest in the other day. What did he do?'

'I had a priest *and* a minister, actually. The priest came up first and listened to what I had to say. Then he told me he was going to perform an exorcism to rid the place of any evil spirits. He held a big cross and rosary beads in his hand and started reading some passages from the bible. He didn't get very far before all hell broke loose. The banging noise began . . . the first time I've heard it when I've not been in bed. But it wasn't just that. The bedroom door banged shut, a cup that was sitting in the kitchen smashed onto the floor, and a pile of letters I had on my living room table scattered across the carpet.'

'And what did the priest do?'

'He left! He looked flustered and gathered his gear together and just went. He apologised, right enough, but he couldn't get out of here quick enough. Things settled down a little after he was gone, although the banging carried on for a while. And then yesterday a minister came to see me. I don't know how he found out about what had been going on here, maybe the priest contacted him. Anyway, I told him his fellow clergyman had done enough the day before, but this minister persuaded me to let him have a look and to say a few words. He was out of here like a shot, too.'

'Why, did the same thing happen again?' I asked.

'Well . . . why don't you have a look for yourself.' He turned round and walked along the hallway, and then stopped before the closed bedroom door. 'Are you ready for this?'

'Go on,' I told him.

I thought the old man was being overly dramatic as he slowly turned the handle, but as the interior of the bedroom was revealed I realised he was entirely justified.

As the sunlight shone through the window directly opposite and bathed over the room, it took me a moment to recognise what was different about the place.

I noticed the shadow on the floor first of all. It took me a couple of seconds to understand the flaw in the visual but then my eyes were drawn to an object above my line of sight.

I don't know why I didn't see this first but there it was, like something from a funfair's haunted house. The bed . . . stuck to the ceiling.

I looked at Harry and the superintendent. Both stared back with a gaze that suggested they were waiting on me to provide a ready-made answer to this abnormality. I took some tentative steps inside, making sure not to position myself under the bed, and stood with my back against a chest of drawers. I looked at one of the wooden legs from the bed, just inches from my head.

As I peered upwards I could see the edges of the single blanket and sheet hanging over the mattress as the bed linen pressed against the ceiling. A fleeting thought passed through my mind that this was a hoax but I quickly dismissed it. Too much work would have been involved for such a bizarre trick. I walked round the edge of the bed, looking at it from all angles as best I could.

'What do you make of it?' the superintendent asked.

'I don't know,' I muttered. One thing I did know was the weak presence, which I had felt when I was originally in Harry's home, was now much stronger. I had a fair idea why. The men of the cloth who think they can perform exorcisms are man-taught – they learn from lectures or books – and it is often a recipe for disaster because they are not physically or mentally prepared for many of the situations in which they find themselves.

'When did this happen?' I added.

'Last night. I was in the bathroom when I heard this almighty bang, different from the usual noise,' Harry said. 'I came rushing out of the toilet and saw the bed stuck to the ceiling. The minister rushed straight out of the door. I was terrified but didn't want to call on the warden or the police or anyone else as it was getting late, so I put out the light and closed the door and sat in the living room all night. I never slept a wink.'

'Have you tried to pull it down?' I stood in front of the window on the opposite side of the room, the elevated bed stationed between myself and the two men like the remnants of a science experiment gone wrong.

'We actually had the police up here this morning,' the super-intendent responded.

'Oh aye,' I said, raising my eyebrows. 'What did they make of it?'

'I think the officer thought we'd been on the methylated spirits, but then he came up with a colleague and saw it with his own eyes. We tried pulling it down but it didn't budge a fraction. They recommended we call a joiner and left looking rather perturbed. They promised not to say anything but it's probably the talk of the station as we speak.'

I asked if he would be able to get a couple of men just now to give it another go. He said it would be a waste of time but I reassured him it was worth trying again, so he left to round up some members of staff.

I had a feeling that if I laid my hand on one of the legs the bed would come thudding to the ground. It was being held up in the air with the energy from whatever this presence was, but I reckoned that when I touched it the actions would be reversed. I needed some men to grab onto the bed to stop it from crashing through the floor or splintering into firewood, such would be the impact.

It wasn't long before the superintendent came back with two young men who, upon seeing the bed, obviously couldn't decide whether they were the fall guys in a practical joke or walk-on extras in an episode of *The Twilight Zone*. Once they had recovered from the shock and were reassured this was most definitely real, I asked them and the superintendent to each stand beside a bed leg, which were hanging from the ceiling like varnished stalactites.

'Now, when I grab onto this,' I said, pointing to the leg at the bottom, left-hand side, 'and pull down on it, I expect the bed is going to unstick itself from the ceiling and crash to the floor like a plane without an engine. Unless you each grip tightly onto a leg and do your best to guide it down, then Harry is going to be sleeping with the rats in the cellar tonight.'

The superintendent pulled the bedside cabinet next to where he stood back across the carpet a few feet to allow him a better vantage point.

Each of the men was at a corner and Harry remained in the doorway, a look of terror still etched on his face.

'Ready, lads?'

There were a few affirmative grunts, about as much as I could expect in the circumstances, so I slowly raised my hands to the leg and the others followed suit.

'Take a grip, boys . . . now!' I tugged on the wood with no more vigour than a young child pulling on its mother's coat, yet the bed dropped like a wayward firework plummeting to the ground.

The men grabbed onto the bed and were forced to the

floor as they attempted to quell the force with which it plunged.

The bang was so loud it sounded like the one o'clock gun at Edinburgh Castle and probably caused every resident in the complex to jump from their chairs in fright, but we had managed it.

The shocked men struggled to their feet and brushed themselves down, checking their hands to make sure they hadn't lost a finger. Harry looked relieved but was as white as his bed sheets, which were creased but otherwise perfectly in order. I looked up at the painted ceiling but there was no indication that a heavy wooden bed had been fixed to it just moments earlier.

After a few minutes the two young men left, followed closely by the superintendent. I told him I'd like to have a quick chat and he said to drop by his office, next to the reception, when I was ready. I took Harry into the living room and sat him down in his chair while I made us a pot of tea. The old boy was understandably still shaken but as he sipped from his mug he seemed to calm down.

I asked him if he would be all right for a few minutes while I went to speak to the superintendent. He glanced towards the bedroom door but nodded his head and assured me he would be fine.

The superintendent was sitting at a wide, wooden desk and gazing out the window to a patch of grass by the side of the complex when I went into his office. He motioned for me to take a seat and gave out a heavy sigh.

'I still can't believe what happened in there. What was it all about?'

'Well, that's what I hoped you might be able to help me work out,' I replied. 'There's something or somebody not happy with Harry living in that flat and it's trying to force him out. Now, this building is obviously fairly new and Harry tells me he's only been living here a short while. So, how many previous occupants have there been in his flat?'

'Just the one. She died a few months ago and Harry was next on the list, so he got the flat.'

The superintendent went on to tell me that the old lady who had lived there previously had been very house proud. She treated that wee flat like a palace and it was always spotless. She had her friends in for tea regularly and it sounded like they were having the time of their lives. But then, sadly, she became ill and died.

It was all making sense to me now.

I asked him if I could use his phone and called Margaret to let her know I still had some business to take care of here, so it would be the morning before I would drive back up the road.

The superintendent thanked me for sorting his extraordinary problem, but I knew the job was not quite finished.

I returned to Harry's place and made us some dinner. We spent the evening chatting and passing the time, and I hoped I was succeeding in keeping his mind at ease as time ticked towards his bedtime, when the banging would usually begin. I told him I would stay the night to make sure everything was dealt with. The thankful old man gathered a blanket and spare pillow from the cupboard in his bedroom so I could sleep on his couch.

A short time later he readied himself for bed, as he was completely shattered. He was wary about going into the bedroom and lying down on that bed, but I assured him it would be okay and if he needed my help just to shout.

It wasn't too long before I heard snoring through the thin

wall. The exhaustion had trumped the fear and he was out like a light.

That's not to say she wasn't watching. I'd felt her presence for quite some time but I hadn't said anything to Harry because I knew it would alarm him. While he was preparing to go to bed I could feel the manifestation strengthening and I knew she was planning to start her games. However, I think she could tell I was there and I wasn't going to be scared by her, because she didn't disturb Harry when he climbed under the covers, as she usually did.

I turned off the lights and spread out the blanket on the couch, but before I too could go to sleep I had to solve this problem for Harry once and for all.

At no point did she appear to me in any shape or form, but I could tell she was there with me because of the energy in the room.

She didn't want to go.

I knew she felt this was still her home, and that she was settled here and had enjoyed good times within these walls. It was a classic haunted house scenario, but it was time for her to move on. There was nothing here for her anymore, she was in purgatory and needed to carry on to the other side.

I locked in on her spirit and felt the energy seeping into my body. It's a powerful sensation at first, and generates that electricity I've described before, but the feeling turns to a debilitating, draining force fairly quickly. I slumped onto the couch, exhausted but satisfied in the knowledge she had passed on.

I had just enough energy to pull the blanket over my legs before I blacked out.

The sun was drifting through the window and Harry was in the kitchen making breakfast when I woke up the next morning.

I adjusted my eyes to the light and watched him pour tea into two cups. The old man looked as if a great weight had been lifted from his shoulders.

'Good morning, Tom,' he said brightly, handing me a cup as I pushed myself up off the couch. The rest had done me a world of good, too.

'Did you sleep well?'

'The best night's sleep I've had in months . . . since I moved here in fact.'

'I'm glad to hear it. You should be having plenty more restful nights because your problem has been fixed, I took care of it last night.'

Old Harry didn't understand what I meant but he didn't bother to ask. A few weeks ago he hadn't believed in ghosts. He did now and he also believed me when I said the issue had been handled.

I freshened up and readied myself for the drive home. As I was leaving, Harry went to a cabinet in his room and brought out an unopened bottle of whisky.

'That's for you, Tom, to thank you for everything you've done for me. If it wasn't for you I'd have been driven demented.'

'Really Harry, that's not necessary. Keep it for yourself and toast a new beginning.'

'No, I insist. Take it, for it's the least I can do.'

I accepted the bottle and placed it under my arm as I shook Harry's hand.

'Take care of yourself,' I told him. 'You deserve to be happy here.'

As I walked along the corridor and out of the glass doors towards my car, I held the bottle of amber nectar in my hand and chuckled as I looked at the label. It was the only brand of whisky I've ever tasted that I not only don't like but that actually makes me sick any time I touch a drop.

'Oh well,' I sighed, as I placed the bottle and my jacket down on the passenger seat as I stepped into the car. I turned the ignition and watched as the petrol gauge barely moved from empty, and wished Rover could use whisky as fuel.

A trip to the petrol station would be the first order of the day before my leaving of Liverpool.

7

The Frightened Seabees

By 1974, my life had changed considerably. Circumstances meant I was no longer able to devote so much time to paranormal investigations and, in effect, I had retired from ghosthunting.

McGregor had moved to the Borders and Willie had started a new job and relocated to Glasgow, leaving little space on his schedule, which spelled the end for our gang. A while had passed since we had last worked together and although we tried to keep in touch as we remained good friends, our lives had simply taken us separate ways. And while the distance between our homes was by no means an insurmountable journey, my work commitments were proving an effective roadblock from getting the team together.

I was serving my country at the time in hostile locations around the world, and simply returning home in one piece was my only priority and proved to be an arduous task. There were a few close calls, but it's not a period of my life I talk about although I am very proud of my military career.

In February 1974, I was on leave, happy to be spending time with my wife and kids in the comfort of my own house, enjoying home-cooked meals and having the opportunity to see old friends.

I had been at the local shop one morning buying a newspaper and when I came back Margaret told me I had missed a telephone call from a woman at a Sunday newspaper. The message was simply to ring her upon my return, so I dialled the number that had been written on a scrap of paper by the phone and listened as a female voice answered and confirmed it was she who had called me earlier. She was a reporter, who I'll call 'Sheila', and she asked how I was fixed to take a trip to Dunoon with her to investigate a supposed haunting in a local hotel that was upsetting the residents.

I paused before answering. It had been a while and I think Sheila perhaps sensed my apprehension because she interrupted the silence to repeat the question.

'Okay,' I told her. 'When?'

'How about right now?' she replied. 'I can come and pick you up in half an hour.'

'You don't give folk much notice, do you? Right, I'll be waiting.'

Sure enough, thirty minutes later there was a screech of brakes outside my house and I peeked through the curtains to see an unfamiliar car containing an unfamiliar woman parked askew in front of my gate. I picked up my jacket, said goodbye to Margaret and made my way out to the car, where I introduced myself to Sheila.

She was a small, slender woman, probably in her mid-thirties, and I quickly learned she had a bolshie attitude and wasn't backwards at coming forwards, so she wasn't unlike many other journalists I had encountered over the years.

Sheila told me we were taking the boat to Dunoon and if we hurried we should make it on to a sailing leaving soon. I ensured my seatbelt was securely fastened and held on to the door handle as the countryside flashed by me in a blur.

'So what's been happening at this hotel?' I asked.

She removed a hand from the steering wheel to reach over to the backseat and pass me a copy of her newspaper. It had been turned to page seven, where the headline read, 'ADAM THE GHOST SCARES SAILORS'.

I gave a cursory glance out of the window to make sure we weren't about to career off the road at great speed before returning my attention to the article.

A dozen hefty American navy men have been scared out of their wits . . . by a puff of smoke. But it's no ordinary smoke – it appears at the dead of night in the Dunoon hotel where they live. And besides waking them up, it floats through walls, opens locked doors, rattles keys in locks, and has even been seen by one man who had his eyes covered by his hands. According to the men, all construction workers with the American Navy, they are completely paralysed when the smoke appears. They all say they can't move because of a weight pressing down on their chests.

Locals believe the smoke is the ghost of an old porter called Adam, who was burned to death in his bedroom in the Crusade Hotel, Argyll Street, Dunoon. The room in which he died is the one where the sailors see the apparition.

Ron Behrend and his wife Elizabeth, from Troy, Kansas, have both seen the ghost.

'I was wakened at three in the morning by the light being switched on, yet there was nobody near the switch,' said Mrs Behrend. 'That's when I saw the smoke. It floated across the room and through the wardrobe. It was eerie.'

I folded the paper in half and placed it on my lap.

'What do you make of that, then?' Sheila asked.

'Well, I've been in this game long enough to know not to make a judgement until I check the place for myself. I certainly wouldn't expect navy men to scare easily, I'll say that much, nor would I imagine they would make such a story up. But let me have a look at the place and we'll take it from there.'

The famous 'Seabees', the construction battalions of the United States Navy, had had a presence in Dunoon for over a decade by this point. This was owing to the nearby Holy Loch, a sea loch open to the Firth of Clyde that measured one mile wide and between two and three miles long, depending on the tide. It's fair to say they had become an integral part of the coastal town.

Just to the south of the loch lies the once popular holiday resort of Dunoon, which certainly felt the impact when Holy Loch was chosen in 1960 as the site of a US Navy base. It was the home of Submarine Squadron 14 and on 1 June 1961, four sections of the floating dry dock, *USS Los Alamos,* were towed into the loch and a crew of 500 Seabees spent the next five months assembling the vessel, which was capable of handling up to five submarines. It became operational in November.

Despite the permanency of the site, there was never an actual base at Holy Loch. Rather, the Seabees were told to integrate into the local area and Dunoon, because of its size and location, became the most popular. The navy men lived in hotels, guest houses, B&Bs and rooms rented from private home owners, while their partners joined in with the local community activities and their kids attended the nearby schools. The Americans opened their own men's club, bank and convenience store, and had their big, gas-guzzling cars transported over to their new home town.

We arrived at the pier quicker than I thought possible and Sheila grabbed her handbag from the back seat.

'Come on,' she yelled. 'Quick.'

She was out of the car before I had unbuckled my seatbelt. Where's the fire? I thought. I hurried out after her, locked the door, and watched as she rushed down the pier at a speed I would have thought unattainable while wearing high heels. As I followed her movements I looked ahead to the boat and saw it was no longer boarding.

'Wait a minute,' I muttered. 'Is she trying to catch that?'

'Come on, Tom,' she shouted over her shoulder. 'I don't want us to miss this sailing. Hurry up.' With that she literally took to her heels and as she reached the end of the pier she leaped off the edge towards the boat, which was beginning to move away from port, and landed safely on the deck.

I realised my jog had reduced to a stumble as I watched agape while Sheila made the crazy leap.

'Aw, Jesus, woman. What are you thinking?' I screamed.

She was standing at the guardrail of the ferry, signalling for me to follow. In that moment I could see no other option but to go after her. Against my better judgement I began running and as I reached the end of the pier I could see the boat had moved off by maybe two or three feet.

I jumped – and here I was without my Superman costume – and hoped for the best.

The best wasn't good enough. I felt my toe catch the guard-rail and knew I was going one of two ways – either head first onto the boat or backwards into the Clyde. Thankfully, my momentum thrust me forward and I landed in a heap on the deck. I shook my head to clear the cobwebs and pushed myself up onto all fours as the throbbing pain in my foot, knees and elbow from the crash landing kicked in.

I noticed the journalist-cum-long-jumper was bent down beside me and I presumed she was checking on my condition.

'I'm all right, Sheila.'

'Eh? No, I've lost my pen. It must have fallen out when I jumped . . . No, wait . . . it's over there.' She rushed away, leaving me in a bundle.

I struggled to my feet and brushed myself down. We had certainly provided on-board entertainment for the rest of the passengers, I realised, when I noticed what felt like 1,000 pairs of eyes staring at me.

I saw two smartly dressed men approach Sheila. Here we go, I thought, they'll have the polis waiting for us at Dunoon. She had the gift of the gab, though, and after a rather lengthy conversation the men walked away smiling and Sheila came over to assure me the situation had been sorted.

I didn't say much. Our working relationship hadn't got off to the best of starts and my throbbing foot reminded me it hadn't improved in the interim. I would do what was asked of me to the best of my ability but I would not be indulging in any idle chit-chat with this woman. I could have been killed or arrested thanks to her nonsense.

My blood pressure and heart rate settled down as I looked out across the Clyde and the familiar sight of Dunoon Pier came into view. It had been a while since I'd taken a sojourn 'doon the watter' to what had been, in my younger days, a bustling seaside resort. My gran used to have a holiday flat in the town and her relatives and their families would take turns staying there for a wee holiday. We used to go regularly, usually on the two-funnel *Queen Mary* steamer. I was quite happy to while away the hours with a cheap fishing line that I would buy from one of the local shops and sit on the pier hoping for a catch. As I gazed at it now I could almost see my younger self sitting there, my feet dangled over the edge.

The boat docked and we made our way off in a much more

conventional manner than the means in which we'd embarked. We walked towards Argyll Street, the garrison-like town's thoroughfare, where the hotel was located.

Crossing the Clyde and approaching Dunoon Pier, Tom was almost in the river in a fraught 'trip doon the watter'.

The sign above the compact building's entrance read 'Crusader', not 'Crusade' as the newspaper had printed. We went inside and I immediately located the bar; I was in need of a drink after the morning I'd endured. Sheila talked to a man and woman while I supped a beer, so I walked over and was introduced to the couple, Ian and Avril, the husband and wife owners of the hotel.

There was a small group of men sitting around a table and I could see they were listening in on the conversation. They stood up and came over to where we stood.

'You're a ghosthunter?' one of them asked in a booming American voice.

The former Crusade Hotel on Argyll Street, Dunoon, where American Seabees were scared to go to sleep after sightings of a ghost.

'That's right.'

'Wow, thank goodness. You have to do something about the rooms in here.'

I asked them for their take on what had been happening and collectively they explained, each acquiescent with one another's statements. An image, sometimes appearing as a shadow, at others as a large ball of smoke, would come through the bedroom doors while the men lay in bed at night and pass over them. Sometimes it would rest upon the blankets, pinning the man to the mattress. It would last only a few seconds and then the dark, hazy image would move away and out of the room.

I assured them I would do all I could to help, as they were obviously scared. Nevertheless, I couldn't help but be slightly astonished at the situation in which I found myself; the famous

Seabees calling on me for help, while I was back on home soil on leave from my own military career.

The Seabees – official motto *'Construimus, Batuimus'* (We build, we fight) – became operational in 1942, shortly after America joined the Second World War. The men tended to be older than those in other strands of the military, since the recruitment process focused on skill and experience. They built bases and huts, airstrips, roads and bridges, hospitals and houses, or whatever else might be required. By the end of the war over 300,000 men had served in the Seabees.

Their immediate impact was so considerable that its genesis was presented by Hollywood in a glossy, rather fictionalised manner in 1944, before the war had even ended, in a John Wayne movie called *The Fighting Seabees*. The real 'CBs' have been a constant in the US military ever since the war, playing important roles in such operations as the Korean War, Vietnam, the Gulf War, as well as the Iraq and Afghanistan conflicts.

I placed the glass on the bar and asked for a look around the rest of the hotel.

As I walked past the CBs, one of them said to me,

'Hey, a ghosthunter from Scotland. Where do you live? A castle?'

I paused and looked at him, trying to decipher from his facial expression if he was joking. He was serious.

'Naw, pal,' I responded. 'I live in a cooncil hoose.'

Ian led me out of the bar and up the carpeted stairs, with Sheila and Avril following behind. We stood at the mouth of a moderately sized hallway, with a succession of doors on the left-hand side but just one on the right. Ian stood to the side and motioned with his hand for me to walk in front. I moved slowly, with three extra shadows following in my footsteps.

I could feel the hackles rise and knew there was definitely

something here. There was no doubting it. As I approached the end of the corridor, passing the closed doors on the left, I was drawn to the solitary door on the opposite side; the source of the energy I was feeling.

'Can you let me in to this room for a look around, Ian?'

'Sure. You know . . . this is supposedly the room where the old porter stayed.'

'Right. Did you know this Adam fellow?'

'No, it was before our time. We've just heard the story,' Avril added.

Ian reached into his pocket, pulled out the master key, put it in the lock and turned the handle to open the door. Even before I stepped inside I could see the room was very small, no bigger than some people's kitchens.

'Okay, I'll need a wee while in here on my own to see if it shows itself to me.'

'Of course,' Ian said, stepping back. Sheila, who stood anticipating entry to the room with notebook and pen in hand, immediately took up his vacated spot.

'No, Sheila. I have to do this on my own. You can't come in with me, I'm afraid.'

'Tom, I'm trying to write a story on this. How am I supposed to report on what I can't see?'

'If there's anything to tell, I'll tell you once I come out. It's vital I'm in there by myself. It might not show itself otherwise. Besides, what I do isn't a public spectacle. Ian, lock this door and keep hold of the key, please. Don't open it until I ask.'

Sheila was adamant she was coming in with me but I was equally unwavering in my position. I moved quickly into the room and swept the door closed.

'Leave it out, Sheila. I'm trying to help these people,' I shouted.

I heard the key enter the lock and turn. God knows what the proprietors thought of this stramash but I didn't let it affect me as I surveyed the pokey surroundings. There was a single bed against the wall to the right with a few items of clothing discarded on it; a couple of pairs of shoes and a large holdall lying on the floor beside the bed; a dressing table with three or four drawers and a mirror in front of the adjacent wall; and a small window on the left-hand side. There were a variety of objects and knick-knacks on the surface of the dressing table: toiletries, letters, a book and a couple of empty glasses. I circled the room as the noise in the hallway died down.

This was the epicentre of the energy I could feel, that was for sure. The place was buzzing.

Some time passed, I'm not sure quite how long, when I felt a change in the room. I was no longer alone.

I turned round, my back to the window, and saw an image before me. I could see why it was often described as a cloud of smoke because it was an indiscernible outline, not a definitive human shape or image. This was a weak spirit and by showing itself to me, and staying there, just feet away, I knew it was looking for closure. It was as if it were saying, 'Help me. Get me out of here.'

As I've become older I have grown more apprehensive prior to an investigation. Not because I am scared but rather because I know what some spirits are capable of. There are those that can be nasty and cause harm or hurt. But then there are ghosts that are merely mischievous and some that are lost, simply wandering with no idea where they are or how to escape their purgatory. Even in 1974, I was beginning to feel more hesitant than in my wanton, youthful days, but in that moment I knew this ghost was not vengeful; it was either lost or rambunctious.

All it needed was a shove in the right direction and I was the man to give it a push. I concentrated my mind, strength and body and set to work.

It didn't take long.

Once I was finished I walked over to the door and shouted to Ian that I was ready to come out.

I paused for a second and leaned my hand on the dressing table, my legs weakened and my strength sapped momentarily, while I waited on the door being unlocked and pushed open. The two women were standing just yards behind Ian, leaning against the wall and chatting quietly. They stopped when they heard the squeak of the hinges and turned round to look at me.

'Did you see it?' Ian asked.

'Aye, it showed itself,' I replied, stretching my right arm out to rest against the wall. 'It meant no harm, I don't think. But it was weak and lost and just wanted out of this limbo, I believe, so I've sorted it out. The men downstairs shouldn't be bothered any longer.'

'What did you do? An exorcism? I didn't see you take anything in with you. I thought only priests could perform exorcisms.' Sheila's mouth *rat-tat-tatted* like a machine gun as she walked towards me. As I've already detailed elsewhere, I've never been comfortable explaining how I do what I do or my gift, and I certainly wasn't about to let Sheila in on it.

'That's something I can't tell you, I'm afraid. I don't talk about it,' I said to her.

'Well, can I go in for a look now?' she retorted.

'On you go.' I pushed myself off the wall and beckoned for her to pass me.

'Avril, come in with me.'

Ian looked to me, as if to ask if it was safe, to which I nodded.

The hotelier stepped back as his wife joined Sheila beside me in front of the opened door, and then both walked past and closed the door behind them.

I let out a long, heavy sigh. Ian asked me if I was all right and I told him I would be; I always felt a little drained afterwards. He offered to take me downstairs to the bar for a drink, which sounded agreeable right about then.

'You better turn the lock in that,' I said, nodding to the key protruding from the door. 'If someone walks in on them unannounced they'll hit the ceiling. They can give you a chap when they're ready. There's nothing for Sheila to see in the room but we'd best let her do what she wants. Anyway, it'll only take me a minute to get my strength back.'

'You're probably right,' he smiled, while turning the key. 'I know how jumpy women can be. I'll pour you a drink and come straight back up to check on them.'

We walked slowly along the hallway. I had only just placed my foot on the first step downstairs when there was a bang from behind. Both of us stopped and turned. It came from the opposite end of the hallway. There was more banging and the sound of something hitting the floor.

Then the shouting began. Now, I've been a miner and a soldier but I've never heard language like I heard from these two women, especially Sheila. There was more banging but this time it was their fists pounding against the door, demanding to be let out.

The cursing continued as we rushed back along the corridor. They were effing and cee-ing, calling me a dirty this and a dirty that. Sheila questioned my parentage, let's just say, but I have my birth certificate so I know what she was yelling isn't true.

Ian unlocked the door and the two flustered women came bounding out, almost knocking us over.

'I thought you said you had sorted it,' Sheila demanded, pointing her finger at me and back to the room.

'So I have.'

'Well, how come that bloody place is jumping, then? Everything was moving. All the stuff on top of the dressing table was bouncing and falling over.'

Ian and I went into the room and surveyed the damage. A glass was lying on the floor in pieces, alongside other items that had previously been upright on the dressing table. Ian looked at me.

'They must have panicked,' I whispered. 'One of them's bashed against the unit there and knocked the glass over. They've given themselves a fright and created a domino effect. That's so cluttered,' I said, pointing at the surface of the dressing table, 'that when one thing falls over, a dozen things are bound to go.'

But upon entering the room I had realised what really happened.

The notebook was placed on the corner of the unit so I turned to Sheila, who stood in the doorway. Her neck was flushed red with anger but her face was pale with fright.

'Did you touch the dressing table when you sat your notebook down?' I asked.

'Yes, I put my hand on it. Everything started going crazy just after that.'

'Ach, that's all it's been. You've just knocked some of the stuff off the other end when you put your pad down.' I tried to sound as dismissive and lackadaisical as possible and walked out of the room, with Ian following. Sheila and Avril looked at me as if they were contemplating murder.

But my explanation to Sheila was not what had really happened.

The moment I saw the notebook on the dressing table I remembered I had leaned on that corner as I waited to come out of the room. The energy from the spirit would have been in my body, which translates into an electrical energy until it seeps out of me. I had left behind this static electricity, I suppose one might call it a *sensation*, which is similar to the sharp shock people occasionally get from a car door.

I wasn't about to tell Sheila this, though. I could just see some daft headline proclaiming me as a freak electro transmitter who zaps ghosts with the energy running through my power cable veins, or some other such nonsense, so I kept my mouth shut.

Sheila wasn't happy with my explanation but she was even less enamoured with the idea of hanging around in this hotel a moment longer. Suddenly, she didn't seem too worried about her story as she told me in no uncertain terms she wanted to go for the next boat.

We went downstairs. I gave Ian my number and told him to give me a call if he, his wife or any of the residents reported anything untoward. I made sure not to shake his hand, just in case any of the energy remained. Sheila really would have had something to write about if I sent a man flying across the room the moment he touched me.

As we left the hotel and headed towards the pier, unable to accept that drink Ian had offered or to say goodbye to the Seabees in the bar, I was thankful that my strength was returning. I was also glad I was able to walk to the boat this time.

Unsurprisingly, there was little conversation on the way home.

Finally, as she drove me back to Larkhall, she asked,

'What happened in that room. Tell me the truth. You didn't really get rid of that ghost at all, did you? You must have angered it and that's why everything went crazy when I went in.'

'Sheila, did you see the cloud of smoke or dark image any of the men had complained of?'

'No, but . . .'

'Well, there you go. You must have knocked something over with your pad or stumbled against the dressing table and set off a chain reaction.'

'I don't remember anything like that.'

'And do you remember some of the things you called me as you were turning the air blue, demanding to be let out of the room?'

'No . . . I was so worked up I can't remember what I said,' she replied, rather distantly.

'See, that's what I mean. The mind plays funny tricks when you're upset or scared.'

We travelled the remainder of the journey in silence.

The following weekend's paper had no story and I presumed Sheila had written the episode off. There was silence from the hotel too, which was a good sign.

A week or two later, I was contacted by another female reporter from the Sunday paper. I presumed the editor wanted something to justify the Dunoon trip's expenses, so they wrote an article about some of my previous investigations and stated I was returning to ghosthunting, having been inspired by their recent haunted hotel report.

It was true. The job in Dunoon had allowed me to dip my feet back into the water – almost literally – and I started taking on cases again, as and when time allowed. Eventually, I became used to working on my own, too.

As for the Seabees, they continued to have a presence in Dunoon and Holy Loch until 1992, when the submarine tender *USS Simon Lake* sailed out, bringing an end to the thirty-one-year era. Nowadays, there is an active community of ex-Holy Loch personnel who keep in touch via the Internet.

As far as I was concerned, while the actual haunting in the Dunoon hotel was of no great note in comparison to some of the other cases in my career (in fact, the journey to the job was more dangerous than the case itself), it is memorable for helping me get back in the saddle and for that aforementioned trip *doon the watter* like no other.

And that's why my return to Dunoon is one I'll never forget.

8

All White in the Night

'Hughie, what did you make of . . . ?'

My words trailed off as I turned from the window where the apparition had disappeared into the night and looked round to my friend to ensure he was all right after seeing his first ghost. The small twin room was in complete darkness and the isolated location meant there were no streetlights to provide even a glimmer over the sparsely furnished space.

Nevertheless, without illumination I could still see all was not well with Hughie as he sat on the edge of the single bed furthest away from me, just as he had moments before when the ghost showed itself. In fact, he hadn't moved a muscle, and as I stared at him now my heart beat faster and a sick feeling gave rise in my stomach when I doubted he could move.

The story of Lot's wife in the Old Testament popped into my head as I looked at this human statue before me. She had stared at something she should not have and turned into a pillar of salt as a result. Was this haunted hotel's ghost Hughie's Sodom & Gomorrah?

His body was rigid and he stared straight ahead. Despite the dimness I could see his skin tone was nearly as grey as the spirit that had passed through the thick sandstone wall. But as I looked at his head, his skin colour wasn't the most shocking sight. What I saw gave me such a fright that I was convinced Hughie was dead. My lifelong pal was gone . . . and it was my fault.

Hughie was just a year older than me as we grew up together in Larkhall. We spent much of our childhood in Morgan Glen, that place of childhood wonderment where we could while away hours playing in the hilly fields, at the viaduct and on the banks of the River Avon, both before my first sighting of The Black Lady and afterwards, when I finally found the courage to return to the scene. Hughie was a good friend, so much so that he was one of the first people I dared to tell about my encounter with The Black Lady and the changes happening in my life.

As the years went on, we both married and had kids but remained in touch. Hughie was a night fishing enthusiast and occasionally I accompanied him to the Avon under shroud of darkness. He fitted fireplaces and was a shop signwriter, but his real talent was more artistic. He was a naturally gifted painter and sketch artist whose work was so good that he often received professional commissions.

Many times over the years he had listened in awe to the stories from my investigations and pleaded to come along on a job. I wasn't too keen on it. By no means was he the only person to have asked and he wouldn't be the last, but I didn't want the added responsibility of looking out for a friend while trying to deal with who knows what. It was different with McGregor and Willie, two men who knew what they were getting into and could handle whatever these situations would inevitably throw up. They brought their own individual strengths to the table. I drew a line under taking along people who may be unable to handle what could unfold, although it was different with journalists; they were there to do a job and I took no responsibility for their well-being, although I obviously wished them no harm.

I broke my own promise on one occasion, and it all started with a quiet drink as I caught up with a friend in the ancient surroundings of Shieldhill Castle, at that time known as Shieldhill Hall Hotel. Situated deep in the Upper Clyde Valley where the sprawling fields and farmland are separated only by twisting roads and rolling hills, the closest village to the expansive building with its landscape gardens is Quothquan and the nearest town is Biggar.

Shieldhill Castle was originally the seat of the Chancellor family, thought to be one of the oldest in the area, that came from France at the time of the Norman Conquests. The tower that now forms the core of the present-day building was built in 1199, but the Chancellors are said to have later vacated the castle and relocated to a newly-built mansion house in Quothquan. However, the family was to return by 1568, after their new home was burned to the ground following the Battle of Langside, an area in the south of Glasgow.

This brief but bloody battle – the forty-five minute clash resulted in three hundred deaths – was between the deposed Mary Queen of Scots, who had gathered an army, and her half-brother, James Stewart, the Earl of Moray, and his men. Stewart had been appointed Regent on behalf of his nephew, Mary's thirteen-month-old son, James VI, who had been appointed king after she was forced to abdicate.

Fleeing captivity from Loch Leven Castle in Perthshire, Mary escaped to Lanarkshire, Hamilton country and loyal stronghold of the Queen. She quickly gathered a thousands-strong makeshift army and a battle with Regent Moray's outnumbered men ensued, which the Queen's followers lost heavily. Subsequently, an order was passed that the castles and abodes of her devotees were to be destroyed and, since the Chancellors had supported Mary, they saw their new mansion ravaged by flames, forcing them to return to their former quarters.

As for James VI, he was handed the reins to the country ten years later and eventually became James I, the King of England and Ireland, in 1603. Two years later, on 5 November, a soldier by the name of Guy Fawkes was found in the cellars of the Houses of Parliament, preparing to blow up the building and all those in it, including James and his family. Of course, in a rather twisted celebration, Guy Fawkes' assassination attempt is still remembered today, with Bonfire Night held each 5 November.

With the Chancellors' new abode reduced to cinders, they renovated Shieldhill Castle and added another tower upon their return. Alterations and additions were made to the building throughout the years, particularly in the nineteenth century when major works were carried out.

The mansion remained in the family until the 1950s, when it was reborn as a hotel. Despite my relative proximity to Shieldhill, I had never visited the property and, truth be told, I knew little about the history of the place at the time of my invitation there to meet my friend, who was a regular at the hotel. As we sat in the bar having a drink and a blether, I spotted out the corner of my eye a middle-aged man approaching our table. He introduced himself as Hugh O'Neil, who, along with his wife, owned Shieldhill. He was an Irishman who had made his money running a big game hunting business in Africa but had come closer to home to try his hand in the hotel industry. I quickly realised he knew who I was even though I didn't know him.

Exterior of Shieldhill House Hotel in the hamlet of Quothquan, near Biggar. The building dates back to the twelfth century and Tom was asked to investigate a haunting that had been spooking residents and staff.

My friend had earlier informed Mr O'Neil of my second career, and with good reason. Hugh feared he may have a non-paying resident, who didn't need a key to enter her room. He told me of the many sightings, in and around the hotel, of a forlorn-looking young woman dressed all in grey, who appeared to be searching for something. Seen around the grounds, up on the roof and inside the hotel, particularly in one room, the apparition was causing some panic.

Residents also complained of a sudden chill passing through their rooms and the distinct feeling that someone was standing at the bottom of their beds. They would sit up in a panic, believing an intruder had sneaked in while they were sleeping, only to find nothing and nobody.

The ghostly girl hadn't done anything that suggested she might cause harm but the sound of the footsteps and the time-honoured 'bumps in the night', independent of the sightings, were causing enough sleepless nights and loss of appetite at the breakfast table to prompt Hugh to take action.

He asked if I could check over the building to determine whether this lady was dangerous or simply a lost soul that meant no harm. At this stage he wasn't thinking of an exorcism, he told me, he just wanted to know whether it posed any risk to his guests or staff. I thought it might have been a case of the superstitious Irish but only an investigation would confirm that, so I said I would check when I was free and would be in touch soon to arrange a suitable date.

A few days had passed when I asked Margaret if she would like to come with me to Shieldhill for a drink, as I had business to discuss with the owner. We were getting ready to leave when Hughie and his wife dropped by our house unannounced. They were passing by and thought they would call in to say hello. When I told them we were going to the Shieldhill Hall Hotel, Hughie asked why since he knew it wasn't one of my usual stamping grounds. When I explained, I saw his eyes light up in excitement.

'Calm down, Hughie, I won't be doing anything just now,' I laughed. 'Margaret and I are going for a drink and I'll arrange a date and time with the owner while we're there.'

Hughie was insistent they come with us, so we travelled to Shieldhill as a foursome and on the way my old pal bled me dry for information on my latest case.

Since my first visit, I had spoken to a few locals and learned of two theories suggesting who this young lady was and what might have led her to wander around Shieldhill for God only knows how many years.

One story was that she was the daughter of a Chancellor

lord and was raped by soldiers returning from battle in the religious wars of the seventeenth century. The despicable sexual attack left the young lassie pregnant and when she gave birth her wee baby was taken from her before she even had the chance to hold it. She was never reunited with her child and died well before her time.

The other tale is similar to the first, except more romantic and all the more heartbreaking because of it. In this version, the youthful lady was said to have fallen in love with a boy well below her class level and when her disapproving family learned of the tryst they banned the pair from seeing each other. But they were too late; she was pregnant. Her parents took the child from her immediately after the birth and, without her lover or her baby, she died, either of a broken heart or from throwing herself from the top floor window of the castle, depending on who tells the story.

In both versions, the young mother is said to have continued searching the grounds of Shieldhill long after her death, looking for the baby she was never allowed to hold.

As Hughie and I stood at the bar ordering drinks, Mr O'Neil came into the room looking pleased to see me. I introduced him to Hughie and our wives before sitting down to organise a suitable time.

As we talked I glanced at Hughie, who was on the edge of his seat in silent anticipation.

'Hugh, do you mind if I bring my friend, Hughie, here, along with me?'

Hughie's face lit up as the words spilled out of my mouth. I wished I could have pressed the rewind button but it was too late.

'Of course, Tom. You do whatever you feel you have to, so long as we can get to the bottom of this,' Hugh replied.

We set a date for the following evening and the relieved Irishman left us to enjoy our drinks. Hughie and I both needed a dram, each for entirely different reasons.

We arrived at Shieldhill the following night around nine o'clock. It was midweek in winter and Hugh told us he only had a couple of residents that evening. Should we need to access either of their rooms he would make an excuse to move the occupants elsewhere in the hotel.

Hughie was excited about accompanying me but he realised it was serious business so he remained professional and restrained, despite the butterflies in his stomach. He stood behind me at all times, quiet and watchful, as Hugh gave us an all-access tour of the property. We passed through the bar and the dining room, the kitchen, the reception rooms, the library, the chapel and the bedrooms.

'It's in here,' I said, stopping at a closed bedroom door at the end of a corridor on the second floor of the old keep, the original section of the building. 'This is where she's been seen in the hotel more than anywhere else, isn't it?' I asked.

'How did you know?' Hugh responded in confirmation.

'I could just feel it. Is there anyone staying in there tonight?'

'No. It's empty. On you go.' Hugh turned the handle and pushed the door open, twisting his arm round the doorframe to flick on the light switch. The room, measuring around twenty by twenty feet, was modest but clean. The doorway in which we stood was positioned in the corner, so I was able to have a good look at the room before going all the way in.

To my immediate left, behind the opened door, was the first of two single beds against the back wall, separated by a bedside cabinet. Beyond them, on the far side, were two small bay windows overlooking the gardens, with a radiator in the space between.

On the wall to my right, which ran flush with the edge of the doorframe, was a small wardrobe, which was empty except for some wooden hangers, and a dressing table and mirror.

On the opposite wall as I stepped all the way into the room was an old-fashioned fireplace, but what caught my attention was the heavy wooden door straight in front of me. I thought it was maybe a linen cupboard, but Hugh explained that behind the door was the castle's original, 800-year-old staircase, which led down to the old library directly underneath this room and then down to the ground floor. On both occasions I had been in the hotel previously, I had noticed an opening in the wall just off to the side of the front door, no more than five feet high and two feet wide, in which a few stone steps were visible. I had presumed this was an original part of the building that had been closed off but, while the staircase was no longer in use, it had not been bricked up. Hugh said the door in the room was locked and never opened.

'We'll stay here for the night, Hugh, if that's all right with you. I feel this is the place to be.'

'Whatever you think is best, Tom. This room has had the most reports of strange happenings: the sightings, the frequent complaints of a cold chill and the feeling of being watched.'

Hugh went downstairs to the bar to collect some drinks for us and, after placing them on the dressing table, he told me to call him should we need anything. Then he closed the door behind him and left Hughie and me alone in the room. I turned off the main light and switched on the lamp sitting on the bedside table. There was no need to sit in darkness. If she was going to show herself she would whether the room was lit or not.

Now adjacent to the hotel's current entrance, the building's original staircase leads to the room in which Tom spent the night, via the door that the ghost appeared from.

It was around 11 p.m. After another inspection of the room and glancing out of a window into the black of night, we each sat down on a bed and chatted the time away. I was glad of the company to be honest because it could often be a struggle to stay awake on a lonesome vigil, and it reminded me of my jobs with McGregor and Willie.

Around three hours had passed and weariness was setting in when we noticed a drop in temperature. I thought it might be due to tiredness but this was a drastic change. I stood up and walked round the bed to check the radiator. It was stone cold and I presumed it had been off the whole time. Although it was winter we hadn't felt a chill in the room before now, perhaps it was because it was the dead of night, but this was a sudden and drastic iciness, as if we had been dropped into a giant freezer.

Hughie was sitting at the bottom of his bed watching me when I felt the hairs rise on the back of my neck and on my arms. I felt something strange, a presence.

I looked across the room and saw a lady pass through the closed door of the old staircase and float slowly across the room. I stood perfectly still as I watched her come in my direction.

She was a young, pretty woman, who I would estimate to be in her early twenties, and she wore a strangely shaped grey hat. It was woollen, like a tea cosy, but stretched down the back of her head to the tip of her neck and was puckered round the front, almost in the shape of a hunter's cap. She had on a grey dress, tight fitting around her upper body but long and flowing from the waist down. Her outline and features were clear and detailed but she most definitely was not solid, con-firmed when I saw a stunned Hughie through her dress as she passed in front of him. Although she was a beautiful lassie, her face was the same shade as the clothes she wore and her brow was furrowed, not in annoyance but in concern. She was a sad, mournful-looking girl. I looked at the mirror on the dressing table and could see myself and Hughie but no one else.

She glided across the room and as she went by me she appeared to pause ever so slightly. It was barely even notice-able. Had I blinked, not likely in these circumstances, I would have missed it.

She passed straight through the outer wall, which was sand-stone and at least two and a half feet thick. I scrambled over the bed to switch off the lamp and then rushed to a window, pulling back the curtains in the hope I could follow her move-ments. Even though she did not emit a glow, I saw her pass across the darkened gardens, floating in a straight direction until she disappeared out of sight. She'd come and gone in a matter of seconds. My God.

'Hughie, what do you make of . . . ?' I turned from the window to speak to my pal but when my eyes rested upon him the words jammed in my throat like a cork in a bottle top.

I was stunned. His slicked-back hair, usually jet-black, was completely white. I thought my eyes were playing tricks on me but blinking made no difference, Hughie's hair had changed colour in the time it had taken for the ghost to pass through the room. And it wasn't just his hair that was white, his face was like a sheet; it was almost as if I were looking at a black and white photo of my friend because the colour had drained from him. I had never seen anything like it before and it ter-rified me.

He remained perfectly still as he sat on the edge of the bed, staring at the wall she had departed through. He's dead, I thought, the shock has killed him.

'Hughie,' I shouted. 'Hughie, are you all right?' He didn't

answer. He didn't even move. My heart raced as I rushed over and grabbed him by the shoulders and shook him with all the strength I could muster.

'Hughie. Hughie, can you hear me?' His hair bounced up and down as I handled him like a rag doll. Every hair on his head was white, right down to the roots.

After a moment his eyes flickered and he lifted a hand as if to say 'enough'.

'I'm okay, Tom, I'm okay.'

The whispered, breathless words barely escaped from his mouth. He didn't sound okay and he sure as hell didn't look okay. I sat down on the edge of the bed beside him.

'Thank God, Hughie. I thought you were away for a minute there.' I couldn't immediately mention his hair in case a further shock really did finish him.

'Naw, I'm all right, I think. How do you do it, Tam? I was terrified when I saw it coming towards us. I watched the whole thing happen but I was frozen to the spot. I literally couldn't move a muscle. It was like diving head first into freezing water. Everything went numb, from the tip of my head all the way down to my feet.'

I stood up and collected his glass from the bedside cabinet and switched on the lamp. I tried not to stare at his hair as I sat down beside him and placed the whisky in his hand, encouraging him to take a sip. He knocked it straight back.

'What did it say to you?' he asked, handing the glass back to me.

'What do you mean? She didn't say anything to me.' I placed my hand on his shoulder reassuringly. 'Are you sure you're all right, Hughie?'

'I could've sworn she stopped and the pair of you spoke to each other.'

'She paused, Hughie, but it was for a second, if that. She certainly didn't speak to me and I didn't open my mouth to her, either. Do you think you would be able to sketch her?'

He stood up, unsteadily at first but he seemed to be calming down a little. The colour was slowly returning to his cheeks but the same couldn't be said for his hair. I was going to have to tell him. He would see it in the mirror anyway, now that he was up on his feet. I cleared my throat nervously and took a deep breath.

'Hughie . . . listen, mate . . . I think you should take a look at yourself in the mirror there. Now, don't be alarmed.'

Who was I kidding?

Hughie walked over to the dressing table and bent down for a better view. I watched him check his reflection and saw his eyes widen, so much that I thought they were going to pop out of his head like a Looney Tunes character. The colour drained from his face again.

'Oh Jesus. What's happened to me?' he shrieked. He staggered backwards and my heart was in my mouth, but then he regained his footing and lunged towards the mirror. He grabbed two fistfuls of hair and stared for what seemed a long time.

'Put that light on, Tom. Do you see this? What the hell's happened to me?' He was livid but not as much as he was terrified and panicked. I switched on the light as he instructed and stood back, giving him a moment to hopefully come to terms with his condition. He leaned in against the mirror until he was almost touching it and twisted his head and neck and pulled at strands of hair.

'Did you see it happen?' he asked.

'No, I did not. I was fixated on her and it wasn't until I turned round from the window to speak to you that I noticed. I nearly dropped from the fright you gave me, to be honest. I

Today a wardrobe is positioned in front of the door in the Shieldhill
House hotel room, from which the ghostly apparition appeared to Tom
and his friend, Hughie.

thought you were away. It must have been the shock of seeing the ghost that did it, but I'll be damned if I've ever seen anything like it before.'

As I spoke, I noticed a movement out the corner of my eye. The section of the wall she had passed through moments before had droplets of water pouring down it in a steady flow covering a width of two feet or thereabouts. The wall was weeping.

'Hughie, I know you're preoccupied just now, but did you notice any dampness or water on that wall at any point in the night?' I pointed towards the section in question. He stopped pulling at his hair for a moment and turned round to the weeping wall.

He shook his head. 'No, that was definitely not like that before she appeared.' He turned his attention back to the mirror and looked at his hair forlornly. I thought he might start weeping, too.

'I need to get out of here, Tom. Can we go? I don't think I can spend another minute in this place.'

'No, that's fine. We'll get on the road now. If Hugh isn't downstairs then I'll call him in the morning and let him know what's happened. Come on, let's go.'

Hughie didn't need to be told twice and he rushed out the room as I pulled open the door. I walked over to the beds and switched off the lamp, grabbed our coats and followed Hughie out, flicking off the light switch and closing the door gently behind me. He rushed down the stairs and out the front door before I had the chance to pull on my jacket. I made my way down after him, hesitating briefly at the unmanned reception desk to look for Hugh or whoever was on night manager duty.

I'll call first thing in the morning, I thought, and made my way into the bitterly cold night, wondering if I might encounter the grey lady while I walked to the car.

Hughie's trembling hand was failing to connect the key with the lock in the car door, so I told him I would drive us home while he calmed down. He walked round to the passenger side, feeling and poking his hair as if it were not his own.

I drove back to my house, where by that time Hughie had settled down a little despite continuing to inspect his hair. I couldn't blame him. It was a phenomenon. He assured me he felt well enough to drive the rest of the way, so we said our goodbyes and I promised to call him in the morning.

I went inside and straight to bed, where I lay under the sheets beside a sound asleep Margaret and stared at the ceiling, going over the night's events in my head. It was amazing to think we had come face-to-face with a ghost yet it had been overshadowed by what had transpired afterwards. I hoped Hughie would be all right. I blamed myself because I had given in and allowed him to accompany me, but I was relieved my worst fears hadn't been realised. At least he was still alive. My head was full of muddled thoughts when I drifted off to sleep some time later.

I woke fairly early considering it was the middle of the night before I had come home but there was too much going on in my mind to allow me to sleep any longer. I was up only a short while when the telephone rang. It was Hughie, and he sounded wired to the moon. He told me he hadn't gone to bed since there was no chance he would sleep, so he'd sat down with his sketch pad and begun drawing the image while it was still fresh in his mind, although I had a feeling it would be ingrained in his brain until the day he died. He'd done a few sketches of her and wanted to give one to Hugh O'Neil. I had planned on calling him soon anyway so I said to Hughie, if he felt brave enough, to pick me up and we could go back to Shieldhill and give Mr O'Neil the picture and explain to him what had happened.

Hughie wasn't slow off the mark and before I knew it I was in his car and on our way to the hotel. I was surprised he was willing to return so soon since he couldn't get out of there quick enough just hours before, but he told me he thought it would be fine since it was daylight. Besides, he added, he wouldn't be going anywhere near that room in any case. He pulled his cap further down on his head as he spoke but his newly white hair was still visible at the back and sides.

'You spoke to her though, didn't you?'

'Not this again, Hughie. I told you already. She paused in front of me for a split second but neither of us opened our mouths.'

'Did you tell her where her baby was?'

'Hughie! Listen to me. I didn't say a word to her. I couldn't tell her about her baby because I don't know anything. I'm telling you the truth.'

He looked at me like he didn't know what to believe. I was beginning to think his hair wasn't the only effect the ghost sighting had imbued upon him.

Inside Shieldhill we located Hugh and sat down with him in the bar. Before I had the chance to tell him what had unfolded, he asked me if I knew anything about the water streaming down the wall in the room.

'I've had a couple of heaters in there all morning as well as the radiator turned up full in an attempt to dry it out. I've been on a stepladder with cloths wiping the wall down, too, but it won't stop.'

I explained what had happened and how the ghost had

passed through that part of the wall. While I was talking Hughie removed his hat.

'Bejesus,' Hugh spluttered in his thick Irish brogue. 'Is that real?'

'Aye, it is that unfortunately,' Hughie replied, pushing the hat down onto his head.

'The fright of seeing the Grey Lady turned his hair white in an instant,' I added. 'I thought he was dead at first, so I'm glad it's only his hair that's been affected.'

Hughie gave the hotelier one of the sketches. It was a great drawing and really captured the young lady. Hugh was impressed. Before we left, he asked me up to the room while Hughie waited at the bar and, sure enough, the water was still rolling down that section of the wall. I could offer no suggestions as to how he might fix it.

I brought up the matter of an exorcism and said I could come back again, if that's what he wished, but Mr O'Neil said he didn't think that was necessary if the ghost wasn't going to cause any harm. I told him it wouldn't, but then pointed out that the ghost hadn't meant Hughie any harm yet he had almost dropped dead from the shock. Regardless, Mr O'Neil decided he wanted to live with the ghost rather than evict it.

So we said our goodbyes and he promised to let me know should anything else happen. I later heard the wall wept for several more days before ceasing as suddenly as it had begun.

As for Hughie, within a few weeks he and his new hair colour were all over the papers, thanks to the story spreading like wildfire locally and beyond. If I recall correctly he was in at least three of the national press titles, all of which sent reporters and photographers to his home to closely inspect his hair to make sure it hadn't been dyed.

I returned to the hotel around two years later, with a crew from BBC Radio Scotland. I was recording a special ghost programme for their Christmas schedule and I told the tale of our night in Shieldhill on location for the show. By that time the O'Neils had sold up and the new owners, two Americans, were interviewed for the segment. Incidentally, when they took over the hotel, Hughie paid them a visit and gave them a copy of his grey lady sketch, while filling them in on the story.

To this day, the tale of the Grey Lady is well-known in the area and the current owners, who have upgraded the building to a four-star luxury hotel while still keeping the original feel of the 800-year-old structure, have used the Grey Lady as a means of publicity and an added attraction. They rent the haunted room to guests brave enough to spend a night within its walls, and often host ghosthunts where people are invited to spend an evening searching for the spirit.

A while after the BBC show was broadcast, I was told a story about a property in Quothquan purchased by English golfer Tony Jacklin. The two-time major winner and Ryder Cup legend had apparently bought the house as a summer home, but his wife had spotted an apparition in the grounds of the house early on in their residency and refused to stay there a moment longer. The description of what she saw sounded very much like the ghost I had seen in Shieldhill and I wondered whether the Grey Lady had gone beyond the confines of the former land of the Chancellors to extend the search for her child.

As for Hughie, well, he slowly became used to his new hair colour and decided not to reach for the Grecian. He continued to maintain that I had had a conversation with the Grey Lady that night and, no matter how many times I insisted I did not, I still don't think he really believed me.

Unfortunately, my lifelong pal died well before his time. For a long time I questioned whether I did right by allowing him to come with me on an investigation, but I know how happy he was to accompany me and it's that I focus on when I think of him.

In a lifetime of shocks and amazing sights, Hughie's night at Shieldhill is near the top of my list of unbelievable moments.

It's an investigation I will never forget and Hughie is a friend I will certainly always remember.

9

The Final Curse

Football. It's the one subject that has the ability and power to tear apart and bring together this wee country of mine more than any other. It is the nation's passion.

Friendships are formed and ruined, family takes a back seat while the fanatic follows his team on the road, personal health is put at risk, but the elation of victory makes it seem worthwhile; the back-and-forth list goes on and on, and it's all thanks to – and because of – football.

For such a small nation, an inordinate number of people spend their Saturday afternoons attending a match. Thousands go to watch one of the forty-two senior clubs battle for victory, while many more take in amateur games, junior matches, reserve, youth and kids' football. From all-seated arenas and plush playing conditions to terraced stands and ash parks, the appetite for the game, in the country of its origin, is unsurpassed.

The legendary football manager Bill Shankly once famously remarked in an interview: 'Some people believe football is a matter of life and death. I am disappointed with that attitude. I can assure you it is much, much more important than that.'

That philosophy is shared by thousands of the Liverpool legend's fellow Scots. And such obsession breeds superstition, among players, managers, backroom staff and fans alike: the player who has to come out of the tunnel last, the manager who wears the same lucky suit until his team finally loses, the supporter who won't go to the game without his favourite scarf.

So imagine how a fan reacts when football really does go beyond life and death: when it takes on a spiritual nature; when a fan believes his team has been cursed; not just a case of 'the team is having a bad run, it feels like we've been cursed' use of the word, but a genuine curse; a spell that has caused a football club to go on an interminably bad run of results.

It was April 1994, and I was in the Applebank Inn having a quiet drink one evening with John 'Jock' Maclean, who was a good friend. Jock was a well-kent face in Larkhall and the surrounding areas, as he was a Labour councillor and heavily involved in the miners' union. He was also a big sports fan, especially of amateur boxing.

In the shadow of The Black Lady's stomping ground, Jock and I caught up over a couple of pints of beer, and inevitably her name and ongoing saga crept into the conversation and the chat took a more unusual turn, as is so often the case with me.

'You should see if you can do anything at Hampden,' he said.

'What do you mean? What's wrong with Hampden?' I had no idea what he was talking about.

'You must've heard the story, surely? No? Well, the tale goes that the Dundee football teams are cursed at the national stadium. A gypsy placed a curse on the city of Dundee before Hampden was even built and although Dundee won the

© PA images

Hampden Park. Were Dundee's football teams really cursed at Scotland's national stadium?

Scottish Cup once, in 1910, the game was played at Ibrox. Neither Dundee nor Dundee United have ever won the cup at the national stadium. The Dundonians are convinced it's because of the curse.'

'This is a new one on me. Why do they think their teams are cursed?' I took a sip from my pint as I shifted on my stool to get closer to Jock, intrigued by the anecdote.

'Well, the story goes that, in 1903, when the football authorities purchased the land where the current national stadium sits, there were travellers ensconced on the site. The hired workers were all ready to force the gypsies off the land so work could begin, but when they realised there was a deathly sick young boy amongst the group they refused. A company from Edinburgh also rebuffed the job offer when they learned of the circumstances but, eventually, a Dundee firm travelled through to Glasgow and forced the travellers off the land so work could begin. The wee lad died and his mother blamed the Dundonian workforce for his death, they being the ones who had shifted the gypsies while the boy was so unwell. So, apparently she laid a curse on the Dundonians, which over time has come to be accepted as a curse on Dundee and Dundee United, since the incident took place on the site of the future national stadium.'

'That's quite the tale,' I replied.

'It is indeed. I don't know whether I believe it or not, but plenty do. With Dundee United being in the final this year, you could maybe do wee Jim McLean a turn by seeing if there's anything you can do about it.'

Jim McLean was the chairman of Dundee United in 1994 and had been, until a year earlier, the manager of the Tangerine Terrors, so called because of the team's colours. It was a position he had held for twenty-two years; a club record. He was a legend at United. He won the league while manager, not to mention taking the team to the semi-final of the European Cup and the final of the UEFA Cup in the early 1980s. Now his club was preparing to take on Walter Smith's dominant Rangers side, which aimed to complete a remarkable double treble by defeating the Arabs.

It just so happened that Jim was also from Larkhall.

The McLean family are perhaps at the top of the list of Larkhall sons to make it in football. A list that could run for several pages, I might add. Maybe there was something in the water in our wee town but, at one time, it would have been possible to fill the Scottish international team with players originally from Larkhall.

Willie, Jim and Tommy McLean were three brothers who all made it as professional footballers, before going on to give back to the game after their own playing careers were over. Jim might have had the most success as a manager but Tommy led the way when it came to playing. He was a tricky winger who played for Rangers for eleven years and is one of the Barcelona Bears, the famous team that won the Ibrox club's only European trophy, the Cup Winners' Cup, in 1972. Tommy also had a lengthy career as a manager in Scotland, even defeating his brother Jim's Dundee United team in a classic Scottish Cup Final in 1991 while manager of Motherwell. Willie was the eldest of the brothers and while his career didn't reach the heights of his siblings, he still had a decent run as both player and manager between the 1950s and 1980s.

There are many more, of course, such as John Clark, who was one of the Lisbon Lions, Celtic's European Cup winning team. Going back further, there was Jimmy Gibson, who played for Aston Villa and Scotland, Tommy Lang, who played in Newcastle's 1932 FA Cup Final victory over Arsenal, as well as ex-Dunfermline, Wolves and Hearts sweeper George Miller. Larkhall was a hotbed of football talent, to put it mildly.

Jock's tale in the Applebank had sounded like an old wives' tale and I told him so. But he assured me that many believed it to be true. Since the Scottish Cup Final was only weeks away I was keen to investigate the claim. As I left the Applebank that evening, Jock suggested I visit Jimmy Burns, the local GP who just so happened to be a huge fan of Queen's Park Football Club, who played their home games at Hampden. Jimmy was much more than a fan of Queen's Park; he was immersed in the club. I believe he might even have been a shareholder.

I contacted Jimmy a couple of days later and asked if he would mind sparing a few minutes with me to discuss a matter he might be able to assist with. It wasn't a health issue, I assured him, when he asked me to make an appointment at his surgery, but another subject he had expert knowledge of . . . football.

I met Jimmy a short while later and repeated the story Jock

had regaled me with earlier in the week. The doc was familiar with the tale and said he had heard it just as I'd told it. I asked if he would be able to organise for me to look around Hampden before the final.

"What are you planning?" he asked.

'I just want to check out the park and terraces to feel if anything seems untoward. I'll be able to tell once and for all if it is just an old wives' tale rather than a gypsy curse. What do you think? Can you help?'

On the week of the cup final, the showpiece game of Scottish football, Jimmy and I were in a car driving to Hampden. Without going into detail with officials as to why I wanted to look around, Jimmy had organised for me to take a walk down through the stands and across the pitch. He was trusted and well enough known that there were no questions asked about my motives.

To add fuel to the fire I learned of another tale of a gypsy curse stigmatising the Dundee teams. This one dated from 1910, after Dundee defeated Clyde to lift the cup at Ibrox, the home of Rangers. Apparently, the prize had been proudly displayed in a Tayside shop window, perhaps an undertaker's premises, bizarrely enough, the day after the win. A passing gypsy is said to have spotted it there and was so outraged that a trophy was on public display on a Sunday, the Sabbath day, that she placed a curse that no team from the city would ever lift the cup again. Between 1910 and 1994, the Dundee teams had reached the Scottish Cup Final a combined nine times – six for United and three for their neighbouring rivals – and had lost every one.

However, this second story only strengthened the doubts in my mind that it was nothing more than superstition and folklore, rather than a genuine curse. Did the existence of both stories indicate it was just fiction, or was it possible that Dundee's football teams had been cursed twice over?

As I made my way into Hampden, I stopped and surveyed the alien surroundings. It was strange. I had been in the national stadium plenty of times but not in many years. It had been altered since I was last here and I had only seen the results on my television. It would soon be transformed again, this time to an all-seated stadium with a 50,000 capacity, although criticism rained down on the development for its lack of atmosphere. Certainly its current form, or even that of 1994, could not come close to the Hampden of my youth, when some of the biggest crowds in the world would watch old-school footballers give everything they had, motivated by the Hampden roar.

When Queen's Park Football Club's general committee purchased thirty-three acres of land in 1903 they demonstrated the passion and popularity shown for the fledging sport of football by starting work on the largest and most technically advanced stadium in the world at the time. Not only that, Hampden was the first international stadium anywhere.

The terraces seemed to stretch up to the heavens, so high that should a supporter be elated enough they just might be able to touch the clouds. It was a much different feeling and layout than that of modern stadiums. Work wasn't actually completed on the ground until 1937, by which time it boasted a capacity of a quite incredible 184,500.

I walked through the rows and rows of terracing, past the traditional Celtic end behind the goals, and made my way down to one of the gates leading onto the pitch. I had yet to feel anything that struck me as untoward. There was a gentle breeze blowing around the stands but it was a warm, sunny day, and a very peaceful and tranquil mood was noticeable within the famous bowl of Hampden.

I stepped onto the green, luscious grass and over the white line as memories of my own playing days came flooding back. I had kicked a ball around the streets and parks of Larkhall for as long as I could recall. I was a regular in Machanhill Primary's line-up and played for Larkhall Academy's team. I remember coming up against the eldest McLean, Willie, during games between the many different houses within the Academy.

I played inside right in my younger days, but as time went on I moved farther back to a more defensive position. In those days, school cup matches were swarming with scouts from the professional leagues and I was one of those lucky enough to be signed on an 'S' form – a contract signed while the player was still in school – for a big team in Scottish football; one of the biggest. I still recall walking up the staircase to an office and signing the papers, in awe of everything around me. As it turned out though, in my own experience at least, my signature on the S form didn't mean much. As far as I can tell, such was the clamour for players in those days that any boy with a glimmer of talent was signed up so no other club could approach him. To be honest, I would have been surprised if the manager even knew I was on his team's books. My brief flirtation with the professional ranks didn't last long, as I enrolled to do my national service after leaving school. I was in Kenya when a telegram arrived from my mother, who passed on a message from the football club that my services would no longer be required.

I wasn't too concerned, considering I was fighting in a war at the time. Besides, football had never been about anything more than letting off steam for me. Ever since that day at the ruins of Broomhill House when I was seven years old, my life had been different from most people's. Let's just say I had a lot going on. So, football was a way of expending energy, letting go of pent-up emotion and aggression, and most of all, an attempt to live a normal existence in the face of increasing adversity and absurdity. My friends knew strange things happened around me. They believed it; they knew I wasn't a freak. That's why they wouldn't allow me to go on camping trips with them. So football was a means of forgetting everything else.

I went on to play for Royal Albert, one of two junior teams in Larkhall along with Larkhall Thistle. Most of the players from the area who advanced to the professional ranks started off at one of the town's two clubs. Thistle was founded in 1878 and is said to be the oldest junior club in Scotland, while the Albert was at one time a senior club but it too is now part of the junior ranks. I didn't play many games with Albert but Davie White, who would manage Rangers from 1967 to 1969, was on Albert's books during my time there and I occasionally played alongside him.

I suffered a fractured collarbone during a match with the Albert but finished the game before going to hospital. I didn't realise it was such a bad injury at the time. It happened in the first half during a collision with an opposition player. I was looked over at half-time and told I would be fine to continue playing and it was only after the game, when the adrenalin had worn off, that I felt it stiffen up. So I went to Stonehouse Hospital, where the injury was x-rayed and diagnosed.

I made many friends through my footballing days and feel I should point out that Protestants and Catholics played together on the same team, without any hassle. A lot has been said about Larkhall, especially in recent years, about the religious intolerance that is supposed to be rife in the town. Most of it is complete rubbish. It's an open-minded and inclusive place where everyone is friendly. When it comes to football, supporters are free to celebrate and sing in recognition of their team's victory. As boy and man in Larkhall I have never witnessed a fight take place over the beautiful game.

I had walked almost the length of the pitch while my mind wandered through bygone days, although I was still alert should anything untoward present itself to me. So far there had been nothing, just my shadow and I in the Hampden sun. I was ready to dismiss the stories of gypsy curses as nothing more than superstition and folklore, as I'd suspected, when something happened.

I was in front of the West Stand, the traditional Rangers end, when I felt my hackles rise. I scanned the stands and trackside but the source of the uneasy feeling was much closer. I was walking near the touchline, almost at the corner spot, when I saw a strange movement on the grass just yards away. I looked to the sky because I thought it might have been a low-flying bird creating a fluttering shadow across the grass but there was nothing there.

I stared back at the part of the pitch in question, about halfway between the goal and the corner and almost on the byline. A small patch of grass, no more than eight feet square, was moving with a ripple effect, as if there was a piece of corrugated metal immediately under the grass.

I quickly scanned the area around me. This was the only section affected. I was just yards away from it but I needed to move closer for a better look. As I did so it stopped, as suddenly as it had started. The bizarre movement had lasted no longer than ten seconds. I stepped cautiously onto the area in question, my foot hanging in the air for a few seconds before I decided to set it firmly on the ground. I kneeled and ran my hands over the freshly cut grass. It was perfect; not a blade out of place.

'It must be a sign,' I muttered.

It, whatever it might be, was letting me know this was real, that there was something here. If the story of the dying gypsy boy was true, maybe this was the spot where he had died, I considered.

I examined the nearby area for the next few minutes then took one more walk round the perimeter of the pitch. The feeling had left me and I saw nothing else that merited concern. I climbed back up the terraces and waited for Jimmy to finish dealing with his business concerns and then we left the stadium and returned to the car.

'So, did you feel anything, Tom?' he asked me, enthusiasm ringing in his voice.

'I did that, Jimmy, I did that. There's something here right enough,' I mused.

'Well, did you get rid of it, then? Is Jim finally going to have the old cup in the trophy cabinet on Saturday night?' He started the engine and eased out of the parking space.

I paused. 'Aye, I've sorted it, so we'll wait and see what happens now.'

Of course, I had not sorted anything. There was indeed some type of otherworldly entity in Hampden but it didn't strike me as a malevolent force. It had shown itself to me, in a form, but I considered it best just to leave things as they were. If either, or both, of the stories were true, it so happened that I agreed with the gypsies who supposedly laid down the curses. It was there for a purpose and it was one I agreed with. It hadn't harmed anyone, beyond causing disappointment for football fans and players, and if that was the extent of its actions then I wouldn't alter the situation. However, I decided the best thing to do was tell people what they wanted to hear and wait until Saturday evening. By then the game would be finished and I would deal with the fallout from there.

Saturday afternoon came and heavy favourites Rangers lined up against perennial cup final losers Dundee United. I watched the television as a neutral as a closely fought match played out. It was end-to-end action but the decisive moment came two minutes into the second half, when disastrous defensive play allowed United to open the scoring. Dave McPherson played a backpass to Rangers' stand-in goalkeeper Ally Maxwell, despite the nearby threat of the Arabs' young player Christian Dailly, and the goalie panicked. He thumped the ball off Dailly in his attempt to quickly clear his box, but Dailly controlled the ball and passed it beyond Maxwell and towards an empty goal. The effort struck the post, but his teammate Craig Brewster was there to tap the ball home in front of the frenzied and delirious United fans. Despite heavy pressure from Rangers, the Terrors held on and finally laid their hands on the Scottish Cup. They were the first of the Dundee clubs to lift the historic trophy at Hampden.

I sat in my living room with a wry smile on my face as the events played out. News had spread round the local area about my trip to Hampden days before and I knew right about now some people would be lauding me for helping Jim McLean's team to finally lift the cup. Others would be cursing me, so to speak, for ending Rangers' domestic dominance.

Of course, I couldn't be sure I had done anything. Maybe my mere presence had settled whatever that was I saw in the turf, but I was not prepared to take credit for the scenes of celebration I was currently witnessing. I did wonder if word had reached United's management and players about my visit to the national stadium and whether it had given them the confidence and belief that the curse was now broken. Their manager, Ivan Golac, who was in his first season in charge at Tannadice, was certainly an eccentric individual. The Yugoslavian took his team on trips to parks to 'smell the flowers' to help them relax before big games and, later in life, he ran a chocolate factory in Belgrade. It was not outwith the realms of possibility that he had learned of my visit and imparted to his players that the hoodoo had been lifted.

The next day's back page of the *Sunday Post* declared that the curse had indeed been crushed and quotes from goal-scoring hero Craig Brewster exclaimed:

'Curse? What curse?'

What curse indeed? Many doubts remained in my mind about the whole episode. The only thing I was sure of was the presence in Hampden that had shown itself to me in that extraordinary but brief wave-like movement under the famous Hampden turf. Whether that was the result of one curse, two curses or no curses, I would not like to say with any great certainty. I had a doubt in my mind and that abetted my decision not to attempt an exorcism on the presence. I have told the story as it happened and will allow you, the reader, to draw your own conclusions.

Oh, and for the record, Dundee and Dundee United have each reached one Scottish Cup Final since 1994. They lost both.

But in 2010, one hundred years after Dundee first won the cup, their city rivals United lifted the trophy at Hampden for the second time in their history, defeating Ross County 3-0. The club's legendary ex-chairman and manager Jim McLean turned down an invitation to attend the game, telling the press that he believed there might be a Hampden jinx over him due to his six losses in Scottish Cup finals while he was the club's boss.

It re-emphasised that those close to the Dundee clubs still believe in the idea of a curse or hoodoo at Hampden.

Me? I think it's safe to say that any curse is now well and truly over.

10

At Death's Door:
Terror on Ben MacDhui

This was the end.

I could feel my life slipping away as I resigned myself to the inevitable fate that had befallen me. There is nothing more frightening than the belief that death is about to take you . . . not even the terrifying encounter just hours earlier that had led to my current condition.

I lay all alone, miles from civilisation and even further from my family. This wasn't the way I wanted to go. Tears rolled down my face and my heart thumped so hard and fast that I truly believed it might explode from my chest.

Wrapped in two sleeping bags but unable to preserve heat, my strength had been sapped to the point where all I could do was lie on the rough terrain and wait, pray and wait. Maybe God would hear me a little clearer here, on Britain's second highest peak. He was all I could hope for now because no other form of help was going to reach me in time. I wondered how death would feel when it finally arrived.

The harsh wind billowed and the rain lashed against my exposed face as I slipped in and out of consciousness. Despite repeated attempts to keep my muddled and despondent thoughts in order, I was hallucinating.

'Dad. Dad, can you hear me? Please, Dad.' It was Elizabeth's voice. Thank God, it was only a dream. I opened my eyes, excited and relieved, but rather than my daughter's image, all I could see in the early morning light was the harsh, rocky landscape. The tears rolled down my face faster now, mixing with the raindrops and sleet that dripped painfully from my chin and rolled off my reddened cheeks.

I looked down into the sleeping bag tight to my body and saw the bar of chocolate I was too weak to chew and the torch I doubted I had the strength to point. I forced myself to lift my head, every sinew in my neck feeling like it might rupture, to look around the spot where I lay.

I couldn't see it. No matter what, I didn't want it to take me. I would rather lie here and perish than . . . Well, I didn't want to contemplate what it might do to me.

Worst of all, I knew this was my own doing. My undoing. At sixty-eight years of age, I had foolishly decided to come out of retirement to investigate one of the great mysteries of Scotland's paranormal history.

Am Fear Liath Mor. The Big Grey Man.

The monster of Ben MacDhui.

The murky, freezing water of Loch Ness may be home to one of the world's most famous legends, but if it's a monster you seek in Scotland, look not in the depths but to the heights of Britain's second highest peak, the mysterious Ben MacDhui in the Cairngorms.

Since the end of the nineteenth century, respected academics and renowned mountaineers have admitted to strange and uneasy experiences on the brutal, unforgiving terrain of Ben MacDhui, which, at 4,296 feet, is little more than 100 feet shorter than Ben Nevis. Translated in English to mean 'the mountain of the son of Duff or MacDuff', it lies on the southern edge of the Cairn Gorm plateau, on the boundary between Aberdeenshire and Moray. It is a harsh, unforgiving mountain, often shrouded in mist and cloud for days on end.

Among the reported instances that have disturbed and terrified climbers over the years are the sound of crunching footsteps; the distant noise of music; unnerving sensations of fear, dread and depression; and, most captivating of all, sightings of a huge, hairy creature, most frequently described as similar looking to the North American Sasquatch or Bigfoot.

My mentor, McGregor, and I would often discuss paranormal occurrences and strange stories that were related to us personally or that we read of in the press. We had a long list of jobs we intended to investigate, it was just a matter of finding enough time. The mystery of what was spooking the mountaineers of MacDhui was near the top of that list. Unfortunately, time was not kind to us and it was a trip we never made before McGregor's health deteriorated and he eventually passed away. He lived his final years in sheltered housing in Glenrothes. His carer found him slumped in a chair one morning by the fireplace, a book in one hand and a magnifying glass to counter his poor sight in the other; seeking knowledge until the very end.

Decades on, I found myself at a stage in life where I realised that if I did not at least attempt my remaining ambitions soon, then it would also be too late for me. I didn't want to have any regrets. I may have just turned sixty-eight but I felt physically capable of carrying out what was on my mind: climbing Ben MacDhui and hoping to unravel the mystery of what had stalked the mountain for more than a century.

*Tom poses at the start of the gruelling walk up Ben MacDhui. Coire Cas
car park and the ski centre can be seen in the background.*

McGregor had noted that the men who had been brave
enough to stand up and relate their experiences on the mountaintop were all respectable, distinguished gentlemen, not prone
to exaggeration and tall tales. Credence should be granted to
their stories.

The first to put his head above the parapet was Professor
Norman Collie, a level-headed and greatly respected
Aberdeenshire man unlikely to indulge in flights of fancy. He
was the first Professor of Organic Chemistry at the University
of London and a Fellow of the Royal Society. A well-travelled
individual, he was described as one of his generation's best
climbers, tackling the famous peaks of the Himalayas, Alps
and Rockies, as well as those closer to home like MacDhui.

It was the turn of the twentieth century when Collie first
spoke publicly of his startling episode on the snowy peak and
he did so to a group of mountaineering friends in New

Zealand. His tale reached the country's newspapers but it was many years later, in 1925, before he recounted the tale in his homeland and caused a cascade of attention from all corners.

While Collie's experience did not feature a sighting of the creature, his encounter is widely recognised as the first report of something untoward on the mountain. Addressing the annual general meeting of the Cairngorm Club, he told the story of his lone climb of MacDhui in 1891.

> I was returning from a cairn on the summit in the mist when I began to think I heard something else other than my own foot-steps. For every few steps I took I heard a crunch and then another crunch as if someone was walking after me but taking footsteps three or four times the length of my own. I said to myself, this is all nonsense. I listened and heard it again but could see nothing in the mist. As I walked on and the eerie *crunch, crunch* sounded behind me I was seized with terror and took to my heels, staggering blindly for four or five miles nearly down to Rothiemurchus Forest. Whatever you make of it I do not know, but there is something very queer at the top of Ben MacDhui and I will not go back there again by myself I know.

Collie's stunning story prompted a predictable flood of interest from the press and public for weeks afterwards, quickly dubbing the source of his scare the 'Ben MacDhui Ghost'. The prevailing opinion was one of scepticism and a number of theories, such as a sudden attack of nerves, were put forth to explain why Collie had imagined the entire episode. But this was a man who had climbed mountains all over the world for years and was used to the loneliness and unusual conditions one might find thousands of feet in the air.

According to Affleck Gray's comprehensive book, *The Big Grey Man of Ben MacDhui*, Collie received a letter from Dr A. M. Kellas, a pioneering Scottish research chemist and lecturer at the Medical School of Middlesex Hospital, after learning of the professor's original account of the story in New Zealand. Kellas was at the forefront of studies on the effects of high altitude on the human system, but sadly died en route to Mount Everest in 1921, four years prior to Collie's public account in Aberdeen.

Kellas' tale of terror on MacDhui was a significant development on Collie's story. He claimed to have actually seen a creature on the mountaintop. Apparently, Kellas and his brother, Henry, were near the summit chipping for crystals when they saw a huge creature, human in form but at least twice the size of a normal man, coming down the hill towards them. The figure disappeared in a dip before they could observe it in any further detail, and they perhaps wisely decided not to hang around and wait for it to show itself again. They rushed down the mountain as fast as their shaking legs would carry them. The episode remained private until Collie's public proclamation prompted Dr Kellas to share his story with the only person, besides his brother, that he knew had shared a similar experience.

For a mystery so engulfed in legend and fantastic explanations, there is, of course, a scientific theory for what so many have experienced on MacDhui. A prevailing suggestion is the Big Grey Man is nothing more than a freak shadow conjured by the conditions, known as the 'Brocken Spectre'. A meteorological phenomenon named after a peak in the German mountains, where the spooky illusion was first experienced, the Brocken Spectre can appear high on mountainsides when the sun shines from behind someone looking through a gap in the clouds. The light projects the climber's shadow onto the mist, creating a giant image much bigger than it actually is, thanks to the lack of reference points when trying to judge its size.

Time was against me, so I didn't want to waste anymore of it and, therefore, immediately set about planning my trip north. My journalist friend, Davy, had a contact in the Highlands who he said would be able to offer assistance on plotting my route. His name was Ken, a freelance reporter who knew the Cairngorms well, and we chatted on the phone at length. I had a map of the mountains and with a pen I would follow the route he told me would be easiest to traverse. I saved his number in my phone, just in case I needed any future assistance.

I'm lucky enough to have had some good, close friends in my life that I can rely on. Mari and Derek Blake are two of those people, a younger couple who live not too far from my cottage in rural Lanarkshire. Derek and I have been on many holidays together and he's also kind enough to do some DIY around my home and help me care for the retired greyhounds I keep.

Mari was visiting me one afternoon when I asked if she would be able to look in on the kennels and my daughter Elizabeth, as I planned to go away on an overnight trip. When I told her what I was planning to do she was adamant I shouldn't go alone. No sooner had she left my house than Derek was at my door, insisting he come with me.

Derek had never done any climbing before but he was fit and strong. I, too, had never been a mountain climber but I had marched up plenty of hills and waded through many jungles during my military career, so I was no novice although I might have been advancing in years. I also live in the shadow of one of Scotland's most famous hills, Tinto.

We made sure we were well prepared in the equipment we

required for the trek. What we didn't have access to, we bought; climbing boots, stove, food supplies, compass, tent, maps, sleeping bags. We were certain we had everything we needed.

On a mid-July morning we were up with the birds and on our way just as daylight broke. We wanted to get to the Cairngorms as early as possible to allow ourselves plenty of time to climb MacDhui at a leisurely pace. As we drove north, I used the time to fill Derek in on some more of the strange experiences of past climbers.

I told him of the varying descriptions of the MacDhui mystery. Some had seen a creature, with estimations in height ranging from eight to twenty-five feet, and hair colour either brown or grey. Others had described a horrific feeling of doom and depression that was enough to take them to a cliff edge, ready to throw themselves to their death, such was the overpowering emotion of despair. I told Derek we would need to control our fears and minds and not succumb to such feelings.

One of the most famous accounts of this symptom was that of Peter Densham, an experienced mountaineer who was in charge of aeroplane rescue work in the Cairngorms during the Second World War. In May 1945, he climbed Ben MacDhui and after reaching the summit, he sat down to take in the view. Quickly, a mist fell and he was engulfed in the eerie conditions. He was too experienced to be concerned with his blind isolation and simply ate sandwiches while he waited for the weather to clear.

Densham heard crunching noises coming from the area of the cairn on the summit and had a sensation that someone was near. Again, he dismissed these feelings as typical experiences of lone mountaineers, but he stood up to investigate the source of the sound. He was aware of the stories of the Big Grey Man but was not afraid; not until he was just a few feet from the sound, at least. Then he experienced a sensation that made him want to get off the mountain as quickly as he could. Running down the hill, he realised he was heading for the precipice of Lurcher's Crag and struggled to restrain himself from running straight to it. He described the feeling to be akin to someone pushing him but he managed to change direction and continued apace until he was well clear of the summit.

His friend, Richard Frere, also experienced inexplicable happenings around MacDhui's summit, but it was the story of a friend that Frere related to Affleck Grey, in *The Big Grey Man of Ben MacDhui,* that really captured the imagination.

This gentleman decided to camp at the summit next to the cairn and quickly sensed a feeling of morbidity and terror. As he lay in his tent, attempting to keep his wits about him, the exhaustion of trying to stay calm caused him to briefly fall asleep. When he woke, he noticed the moonlight streaming into his tent through a crack in the flysheet. But the white light suddenly turned brown and he realised there was something near his tent. As the shadow moved on, Frere's friend shook himself from his frozen state and looked out of the tent to see a brown-haired creature with a disproportionately large head, thick neck, wide shoulders and a height of between twenty-four and thirty feet.

Then there was Alexander Tewnion, a mountaineer who claimed to have shot three times at the Grey Man with his revolver in October 1943. Tewnion had spent ten days climbing alone, and during a dark and gloomy day on MacDhui he heard footsteps coming towards him. When he looked up, he claimed to see a strange shape charging at him. Immediately,

Tewnion drew his revolver and shot at the shape three times, but when it failed to have any impact on the creature's course, Tewnion took flight and scampered downhill.

In an edition of *The Scots Magazine* fifteen years after the incident, Tewnion said, 'You may ask, was it really the *Fear Liath Mor*? Frankly, I think it was . . . for on that day I am convinced I shot the only *Fear Liath Mor* my imagination will ever see.'

That final sentence raises doubts about whether he believed he had actually seen anything real. Indeed, by 1966, eight years after that article was published, he had decided the sighting was nothing more than a combination of mist and imagination. As far as Tewnion was concerned, the latter was to blame for all accounts of the Big Grey Man. Perhaps the interest in his story in the aftermath since it was made public had humiliated him and he decided it best just to draw a line under it all. Or maybe he really did believe he had invented the whole episode.

The captivating tales ensured the journey passed by quickly. We made good time and arrived at the Coire Cas car park, at the foot of the Cairngorms, in a little under three hours. This was the main destination for those travelling to the mountains, either for climbing or skiing. It was also the leaving point for the funicular railway that carries passengers 400 feet up the mountain to the upper station. We considered taking the train to shorten our climb but we were told they didn't allow anyone to go walking upwards from the station so it was pointless, not to mention expensive. Ken had told me the best way to go was by walking alongside the railway track then climbing over a dyke at the top that would set us on our way.

There were probably only around five or six parked cars

when we arrived. The weather was already looking good as we prepared ourselves for the energy-sapping journey we were about to embark on. We each had a cup of tea from my flask and sat in the car eating breakfast, twisting our necks and shielding our eyes from the bright morning sun to squint out of the window at the daunting image that lorded over us. When we were finished eating we changed into our climbing boots and double-checked we had everything we might need. I took a piece of paper from the glove box and wrote a note that had our names, where we were going, and the time we expected to return the next day. I slipped it under the window wiper as a precaution should anything go wrong, before strapping the smaller of the two rucksacks onto my back. Finally, I picked up my walking poles.

I was ready for my final investigation.

We bypassed the visitor centre and railway station, and took the first steps on our momentous walk, unclear of what we may have encountered by the time we made our descent. It was very warm as we set off and the sun shone down on us but I knew it was likely to change the higher we climbed. Derek had the bulk of the weight on his back and we walked at a steady pace, stopping for a rest when needed. We followed the path alongside the railway track as far as we could, then it opened up and we walked across wide-reaching spaces. The views were magnificent but everything was so massive that it made us feel miniscule, mere dots on the landscape, somewhat powerless and at the mercy of nature. Occasionally, other climbers would pass us but not often enough to wipe out our shared feeling of isolation.

The weather took a turn for the worse. Thick clouds engulfed the sun and there was a cold bite in the air. The terrain had become boulder strewn and I couldn't help but feel I had wandered into a bygone age the further we ascended. Modern life has yet to impact significantly upon the Cairngorms and hopefully it never will, as there are too few untouched and unspoiled places left in this world. We were forced to slow down as we negotiated the uneven surface and I continually reminded Derek, who was doing well on his first climb, to be aware of our surroundings and look out for any significant landmarks, such as a number of small cairns we passed by, that we could remember should we lose our bearings on the descent.

We had been climbing on rough, uneven ground for several hours and despite our leisurely pace, I was feeling tired. It was mid-afternoon and the weather was closing in fast. The wind was picking up and the rain was starting to come down. We were near the peak but with the change in conditions and my lethargy, Derek and I decided not to climb any higher, at least for now. We agreed to move a little down the mountain and set up camp while we waited to see if the weather would clear. We walked a short distance from a ledge, where there was a pillar of rock at our side and back that would provide a modicum of shelter from the gusts of wind. We eased the rucksacks from our aching shoulders. I sat down for a few minutes, hoping the rest would alleviate the pain in my leaden legs. Meanwhile, Derek began unloading the contents of the rucksacks onto the ground. I struggled to my feet and helped him erect the two-man Arctic dome tent. Once it was up, we placed our belongings inside and set up the camp stove for dinner. We were famished.

The wind and rain continued to storm around us as we ate our much needed meal. I felt a little better having eaten and rested but still not at my best.

The weather did improve but by that time we felt it was

not worthwhile uprooting. I didn't believe it was a prerequisite to be at the summit cairn in order to see the Grey Man; he had been spotted on various points of MacDhui over the years, so we decided to spend the night at this spot and allow Fate to decide whether we would experience the mysteries of the mountain.

We unrolled our sleeping bags and made ourselves comfortable. It was a cold night; we could only imagine how bitter it must be in winter. We drank tea and attempted to keep the tent warm, and passed time by talking and reminiscing. We were relaxed but aware of our surroundings at all times. Occasionally, we would hear noises beyond the thin canvas walls of the tent, but nothing that struck us as being out of the ordinary. There was no doubting it was a creepy place, but it was pointless letting our imaginations make a difficult situation worse.

It was after midnight when we turned off the lamp and settled down. It was important we tried to have a good rest to re-energise ourselves for the morning descent. Perhaps it was the unusual feeling of being outdoors or the low temperature but our tiredness didn't immediately translate to sleep.

I remember struggling to see the hands of my watch using the limited moonlight that shone through the air vent at the top of the tent. It looked to be around 1:15 a.m. I had been dozing intermittently for an hour. I looked over to Derek, whose eyes were closed, and I shuffled in the confines of the zipped sleeping bag and rubbed my feet together. As is so often the case when struggling to fall asleep, my mind wandered. I thought of Elizabeth home alone and wondered if the greyhounds had caused any problems for Mari. I imagined holidays I would still like to take and I thought of McGregor and what he would make of . . .

What was that sound? My mind came back to the here and now in a flash. I lifted my head and listened. There it was again. Unmistakable.

Footsteps: slow and steady; getting louder; coming closer. My eyes bulged and my heart raced ten to the dozen. Maybe it was someone else who was camping on the mountain. Perhaps they were in trouble. But then again, it could be a joker trying to scare us. Louder again. Moving nearer. I listened to the steps. They were heavy and deliberate. I looked at Derek again. His eyes were wide open and staring at me. Neither of us said a word.

I could hear a mumbling noise, a phlegmy, grunting sound. Not what I would expect to hear from a human. Maybe there was a gorilla outside, I found myself thinking, but dismissed those thoughts as foolish. But what was the alternative and was it any saner?

I grabbed the Swiss army knife I had by my side. I flipped it open and recalled my military training to quickly explain to Derek where to stab a hand in order to damage tendons and render a person's grip useless. No sooner had I handed him the knife than the tent darkened. The light of the moon had disappeared, blocked out by a huge looming shadow. It was enormous; an upright, human form but bigger and wider than any person could possibly be. This thing must have been at least nine feet tall, never mind the shadow it projected. It was moving around our tent, as if it were circling its prey. I looked up at the air vent and saw hair as the creature passed. Grey hair, maybe, but I couldn't be sure in the dim light.

As we struggled and failed to free ourselves from the constraints of the sleeping bags, all hell broke loose. I looked to my right and saw the outline of the creature's two massive legs on the other side of the tent, just inches from me. Then a thundering blow came down on top of us. The tent buckled and creaked. Another whack. Its long arms stretched over the top of the tent and came down on Derek's side. He jumped as the canvas pushed down onto him. The creature made no sound as it attacked but we screamed and yelled like the defenceless girl in a horror movie. Complete panic filled the tiny tent. We buried our heads in our arms and waited for the inevitable. We were tossed from side to side as the brutal blows from the creature rained down on all sides. I felt it brush against my toes. I was aware of the canvas closing in on me as the tent wobbled and shook.

Then it stopped. As suddenly as the attack had begun, it was all over. I lifted my head slightly and looked around the base of the tent. I could see no sign of the creature. I turned to Derek, who slowly raised his head, perhaps surprised to be alive. I could feel my body pulsate as my heart beat hard against my chest, like a battering ram pounding against a door. We were breathing heavily, almost hyperventilating. I tried to calm myself and listened for the creature's garbled drone or the noise of footsteps, but all I could hear was the heavy pulsing sound in my ears. My God, had we found what we came for! I wasn't sure why it had stopped but I was glad it had. I was also well aware it could have ended our lives whenever it chose.

After a few moments I sat up, my head brushing against the sagging roof. I looked around. The tent was half the size it had been just a moment earlier; it was buckled and mis-shapen and the canvas was ripped and shredded in several places. I suddenly felt claustrophobic and brazenly kicked my way out of the sleeping bag. I knew I couldn't go any further, for fear of that monster still being out there, so I closed my eyes and breathed deeply. I turned to Derek, who looked like he had seen a ghost. It was no ghost, of that I could be sure. The destruction around us was proof of that.

The Big Grey Man was a real, physical presence. We were feeling those sensations of dread and fear that past climbers had mentioned, but there was no doubting why we felt this way. I clutched his shoulder reassuringly, unable to find any words that could convey what I wanted to say. Well, there were a few four-letter words that would have gone some way but they had been screamed repeatedly moments earlier.

Derek struggled from his sleeping bag, brought his knees to his chest and clasped his hands around his shins.

In all my years I had never experienced anything remotely like what had just happened. I reached over to my rucksack and fished inside for my water bottle. I flipped the cap. The clicking sound amplified in the night silence and sounded like a gun being cocked. I took a sip of water and then passed the bottle to Derek, who grabbed it without saying a word and took a long drink before handing it back.

The most obvious option at this juncture, while we were still controlled by panic, would have been to escape the remains of our battered tent and flee as far down the mountain as we possibly could. But would attempting to descend through such rocky terrain in the pitch dark, with muddled minds and shaking legs, have been any safer than waiting it out in the tent? That was my concern and I voiced it to Derek. We weren't too far from a cliff and I didn't feel comfortable tackling the walk with just a torch and the moonlight to light our way. I told him I thought we should try to calm down, bide our time in the tent, and make a move at the first sign of light. He was unsure whether that was a brave or stupid decision. On one hand, it left us like sitting ducks, but he also recognised the extreme danger of traversing the mountain in the dark. I told him the beast could have done whatever it wanted, but it had chosen to leave after roughing us up and giving us a scare. I doubted it would come back, but then I wasn't accustomed to putting myself in the mind of whatever the hell this was.

So it was agreed. We would lay low in our tent, literally and figuratively, until daylight. I estimated that would be between two and three hours.

We didn't say much during that time. We certainly didn't sleep. As the minutes passed slowly the weather turned again. The wind became stronger and tested our hole-strewn bolt-hole to the limit. The rain came down, sporadically at first but eventually heavy and constant. Our tent was unable to shield us from the conditions, so we toiled and squirmed into our outdoor clothes and pulled on our climbing boots so we were at least dressed for the weather.

Those hours seemed endless, but eventually I peered through a rip in the canvas and have never been so relieved to see the first signs of light through the rain and sleet. It wasn't much but it was enough to free us from our self-imposed prison. We hastily rolled up the sleeping bags and stuffed them into a rucksack, gathered up the rest of our belongings, and slithered out of the tent into the harsh early morning climate. We were already wet but it wouldn't take long until we were soaked to our skin. I struggled to my feet and strapped on the rucksack.

I looked around the landscape as Derek crawled from the tattered tent. We were in the clear, as best I could tell. As I took the first tentative steps to what I prayed would lead to our safe passage off the mountain, I looked down to the ground to be sure of my footing. I came to an abrupt halt as my eyes locked on the impression before me. Just a few feet away was what appeared to be a giant footprint.

I instantly recalled the story of James Alan Rennie, who was walking in the lower Speyside area in December 1952 when he spotted a trail of massive footprints in the snow. While a photograph of the Grey Man has, so far, remained elusive, Rennie came closest when he took a picture of what might have been the creature's massive footsteps. He estimated the prints were nineteen inches long and fourteen inches wide, while around seven feet separated each stride. He followed the tracks for around half a mile, before running down the mountain to retrieve his camera before night fell or the prints disappeared.

Unlike those he showed the pictures to, Rennie was not in the least shocked by what he had seen, at least in retrospect. He believed the prints were not those of a massive, unknown creature but rather a natural phenomenon caused by a freak current of warm air mixing with the low temperature. He said this created condensation that dropped onto the ground in blobs of water and made what appeared to be massive footprints. Rennie's explanation fell on deaf ears more often than not, and while the pictures are still remembered today, the photographer's rationalisation, which some would find as hard to comprehend as the monster theory, is not.

As I stood agape above the impression, I struggled to believe it could be anything but a footprint. I looked further ahead and saw another three or four imprints before they stopped. Derek was beside me, shaking his head in disbelief. I placed one of my walking poles beside the first print. The pole was around three feet long and the footprint measured three-quarters of its length. The print's width was maybe a little under half this size. I had never seen anything like it. I reached

The huge footprint Tom spotted just feet from his tent on Ben MacDhui.
His walking stick is positioned next to the print to demonstrate its size.
The tent had been destroyed during the night by a creature Tom believes
was the Big Grey Man.

into my jacket pocket and grabbed my disposable camera. I took a quick snap of the footprint and ushered an open-mouthed Derek onwards. As if we needed any reminding, these massive prints demonstrated the enormity of the creature. We weren't sticking around any longer. If the Grey Man were to grab either of us we would have been a mere finger buffet. The scene would have resembled King Kong on the Empire State Building, and one of us would be playing the role of Ann Darrow.

We found ourselves walking with speed, the fear pushing us along. The visibility wasn't good. The rain and sleet lashed down, soaking us. At times it was tough to see what was underfoot but the knowledge of what could have been was enough to spur us on.

I felt lethargic. I'm not sure how far we had walked but in

the grand scheme of things it was not too long. I put it down to the lack of sleep at first, coupled with the walk up the mountain the day before, but it wasn't a normal tiredness. The fright in the tent couldn't have helped, of course.

I looked down at my hands and saw they were shaking. I was doing all I could to stop my knees from knocking together. This was nothing to do with the temperature. Then a crippling pain shot between my shoulder blades and through to my chest, as if someone had lanced me. My God, it hurt. What was happening?

Derek was leading the way and I told him to slow down. No sooner had the words passed my lips than I felt lightheaded and knew I had to sit down before I was put down. I didn't make it. My legs turned to rubber and I fell to the ground. My rucksack prevented my head from pounding against the boulders as Derek rushed to me, in a panic. I lay on the cold, wet surface, the pain in my chest excruciating.

He asked what was wrong and I told him I didn't know. I described the pains.

'I can't go any further. You'll have to go for help,' I told him. He ran his hands through his dripping wet hair and said he had known this would happen; that I was too old to be taking on such a climb. He didn't want to leave me but I told him he must. I felt my eyes drooping shut. I shook myself awake. Derek was adamant he was going nowhere, especially with the Grey Man confirmed to us.

'Listen,' I said weakly. 'There's no use in you waiting here with me. I need help. You need to go down the mountain and alert the emergency services.'

He was frantic with worry but finally agreed. Before he left he tried to protect and prepare me as best he could. He pulled out the sleeping bags from the rucksack and put me into one, then pulled the second bag over the first. He slipped the bottle of water, a chocolate bar and a torch inside the interior sleeping bag and said he would be as fast as he could. I told him to look out for the landmarks and markers I had pointed out on the ascent. They would be his guide on the route down.

From my horizontal position I watched Derek rush out of sight, the rain and sleet quickly shrouding his figure. I was at a low ebb and my cynical side said he wouldn't make it down in time; he wasn't a climber and there were too many obstacles to overcome. I just had to pray no harm would come to him. He was only in his thirties and had a young family to care for. I didn't want the rescuers to come across two bodies in the cold light of day.

That was the fate I believed had befallen me. I thought the worst was coming my way. I had never known a feeling like it; the pain, the lethargy and exhaustion. I was a goner.

Time moved slowly. I slipped in and out of consciousness. I thought I heard noises around me. Voices, then footsteps. A heavy presence. *God, please don't let it see me. Don't let it take me.* I passed out again.

What was that? A helicopter. I opened my eyes. The sound ceased. I was hearing things, hallucinating. My mind was no longer my own. At times, I felt like I had stepped out of my body and that this was all a dream. But the pain in my chest reminded me it was very real.

I wondered if eating some chocolate would provide me with a little energy. I reached down and put my hand on the sealed wrapper. I picked at it slowly, my frustration growing with every failed attempt. Eventually, I created enough of an opening to squeeze a soft piece through the wrapper. I placed it in my mouth but after a couple of weak chews I realised I no longer had the strength to perform even this most simple of tasks. I allowed it to melt in my mouth, taking a sip of water to swallow it over.

I had lost all concept of time. I knew if I could see it through I would be in for a long wait before help arrived. But lying there alone in those harsh conditions, with the awful pain and the sense that my life was slipping away . . . well, the seconds felt like minutes and the minutes like hours.

As this unknown time moved slowly on and the day became clearer, I made the foolish decision that I would have to attempt to climb down the mountain on my own. I had managed to swallow some chocolate and it gave me a slight boost of energy, even if I did feel at death's door.

I pulled the zip down on the sleeping bag and pushed it off, then did the same with the second one. I brushed the torch, water and chocolate aside and kneeled on all fours. I pushed my hands off the ground. The rain ran down my neck and spine, causing me to shiver. I had never known such an effort just to stand. Finally upright, I tried to take some steps forward but I found myself flapping and struggling around like a drunkard. I faltered back to the sleeping bags, where I staggered inside one and pulled the zip up. I tried to pull the other one over me but I had expended my remaining tiny amount of energy on attempting to move moments before.

I had nothing left.

The tears started to flow. I couldn't help it. I lay sobbing and prayed for a miracle. I must have passed out again. Every time I regained consciousness I opened my eyes hoping it was all a bad dream, but here I was in my living nightmare. I was so cold. The skin on my face was red raw, my feet were stinging and I could barely feel my hands.

Then, like spitfires appearing in the sky, two men rushing up the hillside came into sight. I could barely believe it. I picked up the torch and pointed it towards them. *Dot, dot, dot, dash, dash, dash, dot, dot, dot.* Once more. *Dot, dot, dot, dash, dash, dash, dot, dot, dot. SOS. SOS.* They turned in my direction and ran towards me. One man was out in front and the other came after him, out of breath. The first thing the lead man did was throw a contraption up in the air that came down around me like a sort of protective shield.

The second man breathlessly asked if my name was Tom and I nodded yes. He asked me how I was and what had happened, but the tears were flowing hard and fast now and I couldn't answer. I was in shock.

One of them brought out what appeared to be biscuits and asked me to try to eat them. They tasted like sawdust but I managed to swallow more than two. They gave me a drink and put a furry hat on my head. They said something about being unable to get the helicopter up but I was still struggling and wasn't able to compute all that was going on. The first man said the rest of the team was on its way up with the stretcher but it would be rough going downhill on it, so would I be able to walk if they assisted me? I told them I would give it a go. Minutes earlier I'd thought I was finished so to be given what felt like another chance lifted my spirits and energy. They stood either side of me and I put my arms around their shoulders. It would be a struggle but I thought I could manage.

My God, Derek had done it. A climbing novice, on his own and in a blind panic, had made it through rough conditions to find help. He had saved my life. We passed the rest of the rescue team, who continued on and uplifted our rucksacks. The men were trying to keep my mind active on the way, talking to me and asking questions. I can't recall any of it.

When we reached the bottom Derek was there waiting

anxiously. So were the police. I was taken into a room where the doctor checked me over. My blood pressure was dangerously high but the pain in my shoulder blades wasn't so bad now and I felt I had taken a few steps back from death's door. I hadn't visited my GP for a check-up before the trip and at my age I should have done. It was silly.

The police officers came in and had a word with me, followed by Derek and John Allen, the leader of the mountain rescue team. I can remember the police officers asking how I had made it up there at my age and, perhaps with a touch of bravado, I replied that once upon a time I could have scaled MacDhui walking backwards. They also asked me if I was working with the press. I thought my reputation had preceded me but Derek interjected and explained to both the officers and me that he had called Ken, the freelancer who had helped us plot our route, when he reached the bottom. There was no one around when Derek reached the base, so he used the spare keys I had given him when we started out on our trek and went inside the car to shelter. He barely had any battery left in his phone, so he called Ken, quickly gave him the details and asked him to call the emergency services.

I added that Ken was assisting us as a favour rather than on a professional basis. With that, we made our way to my car. I never mentioned the Grey Man to the police, rescuers or John Allen. They would have thought I was still suffering from my bad turn and would have sent me to hospital. I knew Derek wouldn't have said a word about it, either.

The note on the windscreen was almost disintegrated, certainly illegible. The equipment was piled into one side of the Citroen people carrier. John Allen commented that we had been well prepared for the climb, while Derek pushed down the seats in the back to allow me to stretch out.

As I lay resting while Derek drove us home, I thanked him for alerting the rescuers in time. He told me he had actually lost his way on the descent and found himself on the precipice of a cliff. He backtracked and saw a landmark familiar to him from our journey up, which set him on the right path, so he thanked me.

I had been in my house for just a short while, settled and with Elizabeth tending to me, when my phone rang. It was a news agency from Inverness, inquiring about the incident on the mountain. I told them I didn't want to talk about it and hung up. I was feeling low and a bit foolish, to be honest. I called Ken and asked if he had passed the story on to the agency but he assured me he hadn't and that the emergency services would have provided the reporter with the information.

As it was, the story made the papers two months later when I agreed to be interviewed by an old journalist friend, complete with my tale of terror in the tent and the discovery of the footprints. It provoked such interest that researchers from Grampian TV, which was making a new series called *Beyond Explanation*, later approached us. They were dedicating a show to the Big Grey Man and they asked Derek and me to go back to MacDhui to film a reconstruction of our horrific encounter. No way, I told them, there would be no return to MacDhui for me, even if I was fit enough – which I wasn't. Instead, they interviewed both of us at my home and I was pleased with the final result, which was narrated by one of my favourite actors, Brian Cox.

Before that, though, I attended my local GP's surgery in the days after my bad turn. By this time both my big toenails had fallen off, which I pointed out to my doctor.

'Never mind your toenails. Look at your blood pressure!'

he exclaimed. He told me I was lucky to survive the bad turn on the mountain; that I had been lying between a stroke and a heart attack and it was beyond him how I hadn't suffered either. He asked what had caused it but I didn't want to tell him. He would have sent me to the funny farm. The doctor gave me a prescription for my high blood pressure, medication I'm still on to this day.

John Allen called me a few days after the incident, which was very good of him. He wanted to check how I was feeling and I told him my doctor was angry with me but I was slowly feeling better. He said Derek and I had been unlucky and I thanked him for calling. I didn't expect to hear from him again. However, a week or so later, he called once more and this time he had news for me. My tent had been found up on the mountain and he asked me what I wanted to do with it. I said just to give it to charity or to a local kid who might be interested in camping.

'There won't be much point doing that,' John told me. 'It's in pieces; slashed, as if someone has taken a knife to it.'

Of course it is, I thought. I told him to bin it, as I no longer had any use for it.

Only later did I realise how foolish I had been. When I told Ken he said he would have collected it for me. He pointed out that we might have been able to give it to specialists to test for any traces of the creature responsible for the shredding. I still wasn't thinking straight and I cursed myself for missing what could have been scientific proof about the existence of the Big Grey Man.

Coupled with my health issues, I was having a recurrent dream that was leaving me restless and weary. It had started a short time after I came back from the mountain and happened regularly enough that it distracted me throughout my waking hours, as well as during fitful bouts of sleep. I dreamed I would wake up and at the bottom of my bed was a towering creature. It was all in shadow and I could make out no features, colour or texture, only the dark shape. I couldn't tell if it was looking at me but it made no attempt to come nearer. In fact, it was perfectly still. While I stared at the creature from under my sheets, I heard an unknown human voice say a word that sounded like 'nefilm', over and over again. When I woke up I said the strange word to myself, with no idea what it meant. I couldn't find it in a dictionary and it wasn't the name of a place I was familiar with.

Eventually I confided in Derek. To my shock he told me he had been having a similar dream but hadn't wanted to mention it out of embarrassment. The only difference was he thought the word he was hearing was 'Nethin'. There is a River Nethin in Lanark Valley and, while he couldn't explain its significance, he was quite certain this was the word he had heard. I hadn't even thought of that because I was sure it was an 'f' sound rather than a 'th' sound.

The strange word took up permanent residence in my thoughts and was at the forefront of my mind when I received a visitor in the form of a Jehovah's Witness. My house is some way off the beaten track so I was always kind enough to invite him in when he turned up at my door. On this occasion I asked him if he was familiar with the word 'nefilm' and as quick as a flash he replied, 'Do you mean "Nephilim?"'

Yes, that was it. I asked him what it was and how he knew of it. He brought out a bible and flicked through a few pages at the front, before tracing his finger over a page until he located what he was looking for.

He said:

Genesis, chapter six, verse four says: "The Nephilim proved to be in the earth in those days, and also after that, when the sons of the true God continued to have relations with the daughters of men and they bore sons to them, they were the mighty ones who were of old, the men of fame."

He told me that Nephilim, translated literally from the Hebrew, meant 'feller', those who felled others or caused others to fall through violent acts.

He promised he would come by my house again soon with some literature explaining the Nephilim and the theories attached to the bible passage. I was intrigued.

True to his word, he brought with him on his next visit some further information on the Nephilim. I learned that commentators had offered a number of suggestions about who and what the Nephilim might actually be.

The first is they were fallen angels who had intercourse with women and produced the aforementioned 'mighty ones' and 'men of fame'. Another theory is that the Nephilim were not fallen angels, but actually the offspring of those angels and the earth's women. Other scholars believe they were simply wicked men who caused pain and destruction on the earth until the Flood wiped them out.

This was all new to me, but I was fascinated by the subject. I was certain Derek and I had to be hearing this previously foreign word in our dreams for a reason. One theory stood out from the rest to me and commanded all of my attention; that the Nephilim were fallen angels.

Could it be that this malformed and hideous creature, an image straight out of hell that had been spotted so many times on the snowy peak of MacDhui, was actually a rogue angel of God, dropped in through the clouds?

There are so many theories out there about the Grey Man. This is simply my own personal theory and will remain such.

One thing I know for certain is that it is no ghost. It spared my life but the fright of seeing the creature almost killed me. I will never return to MacDhui and I changed forever the moment I took those first fateful steps onto Scotland's most mysterious mountain.

I warn anyone to think twice before climbing that horrific peak because mark my words . . . whatever it is, the Big Grey Man of Ben MacDhui is real. Very real.

11

Thriller: The Strange Case of the Lochmaben Vampire and the King of Pop

Given the nature of my unique work and the length of time I've been involved, very little surprises me, and even less has the ability to actually scare. But an investigation late on in my career did, on both counts.

Looking at it now, I still find it hard to comprehend and, at eleven years, it was my longest case with the exception of The Black Lady. The twists and turns left me speechless more often than the rest of my career combined and the conclusion literally came straight out of Hollywood.

It all began in 1991, in a small but historically important town in the Scottish borders called Lochmaben. Rumoured to be the birthplace of Robert the Bruce, the town is four miles west of Lockerbie and is said to have been one of the earliest inhabited spots in Britain owing to its strategic location between Scotland, England and Ireland. This would also make it a pivotal geographical spot in later centuries when Scotland and England were at war, making it a suitable location for castles.

In the final years of the thirteenth century, Edward I ordered a second castle to be built in Lochmaben, the castle I would soon become familiar with. Despite being unfinished by the time of an attack by the Bruces in mid-1299, the English managed to withstand the onslaught and work was completed on the castle early in the 1300s. Soon after, in 1306, Bruce's men attacked the castle again and this time they were successful. The English then won it back before surrendering it to the Scots at the Battle of Bannockburn in 1314. Over the next couple of centuries, ownership switched hands a few more times, and the castle last saw action in 1588, when James VI, King of Scots, captured it from the Maxwell family.

After the Union of Crowns in 1603, when James VI became James I of England and the countries shared a monarch, there was no need for such a castle and the fortress fell into a state of disuse and, eventually, disrepair.

I was approached in 1991 because locals were worried about the increasing number of animal corpses found in the woods around the remains of Lochmaben Castle and the surround-ing Castle Loch. They said that in the dead of night animal screams were audible and the carcasses of wildlife – birds, rabbits and squirrels, to name a few – were being found dead by walkers.

It didn't immediately sound like a paranormal matter. To me, the most likely explanation was an increase in the indig-enous fox population, or perhaps a more unusual theory would be a big cat, of which there have been many sightings in recent years throughout Scotland. But as a goodwill gesture to the gentlemen, I told them I would take a drive to Lochmaben and have a look around to see if I could determine what was behind the deaths.

I made the hour's drive to the Borders one evening soon afterwards. The castle is located about a mile from the town and is reached by navigating along a minor road that eventu-ally becomes little more than a rough track. Turning a corner and steering through a narrow gate, the first part of the fenced-off castle that becomes visible is an uncompromising looking wall measuring around fifteen feet in height. To the north of the high defensive wall, all that remains is a disjointed collection of craggy walls and broken stones. Between the edge of its northern point and the loch – the castle was built on a promontory from the southern shore of Castle Loch, which stretches around three sides of the structure – is a small car park, where I parked and faced into the woods.

I picked up my torch from the passenger seat, locked up and made my way towards the dark shroud of trees. It was still light overhead but as I stepped under the canopy of branches the darkness enveloped me and I was forced to switch on the torch.

By shining the torchlight all around I could see there were many paths trodden into the long grass by walkers and I chose one at random, which took me past the castle and by the loch. I didn't see anything at all unusual in among the centuries-old trees but I took due time and diligence just to make sure.

Around half an hour had passed and I hadn't seen anything unusual in the woods. In fact, I hadn't seen anything at all, not even so much as a field mouse. I decided I'd spent enough time checking the area since not once had I felt a sensation that something spiritual might be near, so I turned back and retraced my steps through the woods towards my car. I focused on the large exterior wall through the trees and used that as a guide to the car park. As I neared it I fumbled through my pockets searching for the keys. As my right hand touched the cold metal of the key in my interior jacket pocket, I noticed out the corner of my eye a fleeting movement pass by me. It was a bird or maybe a bat, I told myself, but I knew it felt bigger; human-sized.

I stopped and quickly looked around. I couldn't see anything.

I shone the torchlight slowly and deliberately up and down the craggy bark of the trees in my immediate area and, just to be sure it wasn't something closer to the ground, I directed the light a little lower. I couldn't see anything now but I could have sworn I had seen a figure rush by a moment earlier. It was no more than a fleeting glance but whatever or whoever it may have been, the woods provided a sufficient hiding place.

As I returned hesitantly to my car, I continued to examine all around me, almost tripping on the long growth as I stumbled from the woods. As I drove home I asked myself if I had imagined it, if my mind was playing tricks. But I was too experienced for that; it was all about self-discipline and being in control . . . and I had been. The incident sowed a seed of doubt in my mind and I knew I would have to return for another look, sooner rather than later.

My wife Margaret was patient and quietly supportive of my rather unusual work. As long as I didn't bring it home, she would tell me, she was happy for me to carry on with my investigations. The watershed moment that prompted this ruling came after a fellow turned up at our house one afternoon, having tracked down my address after reading about me in the press. I was at my day job and when Margaret answered the door she was greeted by the sight of a clearly delusional man wishing to speak with me. Regardless that I couldn't provide the sort of help he needed, he told my stunned wife that he was the reincarnation of a centuries-old king and he needed to speak with me immediately. That announcement was enough for Margaret to send him packing with a few choice words ringing in his ears and the King was left with no doubt that he had wandered into the wrong kingdom on this occasion.

I didn't escape her fury either. Oh no. The moment I walked through that same door later in the day I received the sharp end of her tongue. Margaret was livid and warned me she didn't mind me doing what I did, so long as I kept my home life separate from the ghost work. It was an ultimatum I couldn't argue with and would try to honour from then on.

When I returned home from Lochmaben, I told her what I had seen and that I would have to go back soon, because not knowing what I had spotted was gnawing away at me. I decided the best course of action was to spend the night there in my car, where I would wait and watch.

Much to my surprise, Margaret offered to accompany me on the trip. I'm not quite sure why, because she had never come on any of my investigations nor showed any interest in doing so, to be honest. I agreed although at the back of my mind I warned myself to make sure she remained in the car and out of harm's way. I still didn't know what I was dealing with and I would never have forgiven myself if something happened to her.

Around a week or so later we filled a flask with tea, picked up two blankets and a travel pillow from the bedroom cupboard and packed them into the car. As we began our trip to the Borders I filled Margaret in on some of the history and legend of Lochmaben Castle and its connection to the Bruces.

The 'Brus' family, as it was spelled then, were lords of Annandale in the early twelfth century, with Robert de Brus, 2nd Lord of Annandale, ancestor of Robert I, The Bruce, ruling the roost. The Bruces' castle was in nearby Annan, around fifteen miles from Lochmaben, the town to which they would relocate.

It was also around this time that they considered themselves cursed.

The story goes that during a visit to the castle in 1138, the Irish Bishop of Armagh, St Malachy O'More, overheard servants speaking about a robber who was to be hanged. Malachy

– credited with several miracles and for writing prophecies of the Popes – asked his host to spare the accused, a request to which Brus agreed. However, when Malachy later left the town he saw the corpse of the robber hanging by the roadside. Infuriated that he had been lied to, Malachy placed a curse on Brus, his family and the hamlet of Annan.

Not too long after the curse was laid down, the plague came to Annan. The outbreak occurred at the same time as the arrival in the town of a man who, it was later discovered, was on the run from Whitby in Yorkshire. It's said that the Bruces provided refuge for the stranger until it was discovered he was the carrier of the plague. Coincidentally, or maybe not so, at this same time newly buried bodies at the local cemetery were being found unearthed and drained of blood. Thus, the legend of a vampire in Annan was born.

Now, I had never entertained the idea that vampires could really exist; the thought hadn't entered my head for a second. Stories of vampires have been recounted for almost as long as man has roamed the earth but, to me, they were just that, stories. Nothing more than make believe and fiction. However, I knew why the locals in Lochmaben had contacted me and not an animal expert; they believed in their ancient vampire tale.

The old story doesn't end there. The locals still hadn't joined the dots between the vampire theory and the arrival of the Yorkshire man, and he too perished before anyone realised there might be a link. His rotting corpse was buried in a pauper's grave but the plague continued to spread.

Two angry and mournful brothers who had lost their father to the sickness vowed a belated vengeance one evening by going to the grave of the stranger, with plans to dig up the body and destroy the putrid remains by fire. When the grave was opened they discovered a bloated body; not quite the wilted, rotting cadaver they expected. One of the siblings could withhold his fury no more and lunged down into the corpse's chest with the sharp end of his spade. A fountain-like burst of blood erupted from the dead man's chest and rained down on the brothers in a macabre shower, and by the time the pair slipped and stumbled their way out of the grave, which was quickly filling up with blood like an overflowing sink, they had come to the sickening realisation they had pierced a hole in a vampire still full of its victims' blood.

Were the numerous deaths the result of the plague, a vampire, or a combination of the two? The Yorkshire man's physical appearance might have prompted some to believe they were looking at a plague sufferer when, in fact, he was the very image of the living dead. The fact that the plague carried on after his demise indicates there was an outbreak of illness but it's interesting to note that it also killed the Whitby man. If vampires ever were real, and he was one, then his death proved it wasn't just a stake through the heart that could end their existence.

The Bruces moved from Annan to Lochmaben by 1166, to a motte castle, the original castle in the town, and close to the fortress in question, which was built more than 100 years later.

Importantly, the tale states that the notorious Whitby intruder had bitten one of the Bruces and he, too, was transformed into a bloodsucker. With the Bruce's Lochmaben castle long gone but the remains of the later castle, which had briefly been held by the family for a short time in the fourteenth century, still standing nearby, was the ancestral vampire of the great Robert the Bruce wandering these grounds, killing and draining the wildlife of blood for all eternity?

I had a feeling that I had been enlisted to prove that crazy idea was true, but it was an absurd suggestion. I had no time for tales of vampires and returned to Lochmaben to end the

The ruins of Lochmaben Castle in the small but historically important town of Lochmaben, four miles west of Lockerbie in the Scottish Borders. The castle was built by the Bruce family in the twelfth century and a vampire ancestor of Robert the Bruce is said to roam the grounds to this day.

silly rumours and find an alternative explanation for what had caught my attention that first night.

By the time we arrived at the castle it was dusk and, suffice to say, Margaret was none too enamoured with the tale.

We parked, walked down to the loch to stretch our legs and loosen up after the drive, and then returned to the car, which faced into the woods. The castle was to our left. Everything was perfectly silent. I had decided to wait here and watch from afar should anything show itself, rather than go creeping into the dark woods again where I might not have a good look at the thing, should it appear.

Margaret fell asleep a few hours into the vigil but I stayed awake, although I struggled at times. I switched the radio on now and again and would occasionally roll the window down to feel the cool breeze from the loch sweep over my face to revitalise me a little. It was hard work, staring into the darkness of the woods and trying to keep focus, making sure my eyes didn't deceive me.

By the time dawn began to break, the haar was rising and the dew had formed on the tips of the long grass. I decided to take a short walk into the woods that I'd spent hours staring at. Margaret was still sleeping so I let her be and slipped quietly out of the car, locking it to be safe.

It was a brisk morning but there was barely a breath of wind as I made my way into the woods. It was a calm, quiet setting and if anything were to approach me, I would undoubtedly hear it coming. I took my time walking up and down the paths, taking in the fresh morning smell of the woodland and loch. I snapped off a dead tree branch as I walked, breaking it into tiny pieces, which I let fall to the ground.

The edge of Lochmaben Castle's car park, where Tom and wife Margaret camped out in their car and staked out the woods in search of any disturbances or unusual activity.

The entrance to the woods from Lochmaben Castle car park, following the route Tom took as he encountered the vampire for the first time.

It was at that moment I felt something. A presence; not spiritual but physical. There was something staring at me. I felt this strong sensation watching my every tense, careful movement. I stopped but could hear no footsteps from any direction; the only noise was the twitter of the birds in the trees. A shiver passed over me. The hairs on my neck and arms stood on end. I turned slowly, looking at every bush, every tree trunk, every clump of long grass.

And there it was.

I stood still. My eyes refused to blink and I swallowed hard to stop the bile rising up my throat. Little more than fifteen feet from me stood the most hideous sight I have ever had the displeasure of witnessing. It was as if I were looking at a walking, decomposing corpse. Maybe I was.

Its face was as grey as granite and its eyes were as black and lifeless as coal. The skin almost seemed transparent except for the thick purple veins protruding from the creature's dead, withered tissue. It was tall but round-shouldered and a hood was pulled over its head. It was dressed in what I can only describe as sacking on its upper half and slack, baggy trousers on its lower half, like those of a clown. But I wasn't laughing.

Vampire.

The word popped into my head and refused to budge, much like my legs that would not do as my brain instructed.

Surely not. It couldn't be. Vampires weren't real. Yet I couldn't shake the horrible feeling that this was exactly what I was staring at.

I was shaking so much I felt I might collapse from fear but I tried to gather my wits and thoughts as we continued to stare at each other, neither of us moving. Should I flee and try to make it back to the car? Should I attempt to communicate with it? As the questions filled my head the creature suddenly took flight, springing up onto a branch and gliding from tree to tree like Tarzan on steroids. It moved so easily and quickly I knew there was no point in me running so I remained rooted to the spot, transfixed and open-mouthed, as it moved swiftly into the distance.

I'm not ashamed to say I was scared. My heart was beating so hard that my entire body pulsed and I worried I might have a heart attack. I finally forced myself to turn and moved as fast as I could in the direction of the car park even though my legs were trembling uncontrollably. No sooner had I began moving than I spotted it in the distance in front of me, soaring through the trees.

Then it disappeared. And reappeared. Away. Back. Away. Back.

It drifted between the trees with such speed that my eyes could not keep up. There was no way this could be human; the speed and distance it cleared with each swoop would be impossible for a normal man.

This grainy, damaged snapshot was the first picture Tom managed to capture of the vampire, which can be seen on the far left of the photograph.

I was worried about Margaret sitting alone in the car, so I forced myself to move faster. As I moved closer to base I was thankful to see she was inside; in fact, she was still sleeping. I unlocked the door, grabbed the handle and rushed inside, starting the engine and putting my foot down on the pedal with such ferocity that the tyres spun on the gravel underneath. The noise and sudden movement woke Margaret with a start and threw her towards the dashboard. As she lambasted me for driving like a lunatic, demanding to know what the problem was, I made myself take a cursory look in the rear-view mirror to make sure we weren't being followed as I drove out of the castle grounds. I doubted my car was able to move faster than the creature even if it was on our trail.

I apologised but couldn't find the necessary words to explain what had made me drive in such a manner. We spent the drive home in silence as Margaret slipped in and out of sleep and I relived the encounter over and over again. When we reached the safe haven of our house, Margaret, still uncharacteristically tired, went to bed, but I was unable to rest easy.

It was the next morning before Margaret felt able to leave her bed. She came through to the living room and told me she had terrible pains in her legs that were so bad she felt she needed to see a doctor. I called the surgery and was lucky enough to get her an appointment that same day. The GP checked her over and said it was nothing serious, just bad cramps, so we accepted his diagnosis although she was still in a great deal of discomfort.

I made sure she was comfortable and settled before readying myself for a trip to Armadale dog track where I had a good prospect running that night. Our daughter Elizabeth was staying in the house with her mum and they waved me off from the bedroom window as I drove away.

When I returned home several hours later I noticed the

house seemed very quiet as I came through the door. I walked from room to room calling on Elizabeth and Margaret but there was no response. As I passed through the living room I spotted the light flashing on the answer machine. I pressed the button and felt my legs weaken as the message played out.

Margaret had been rushed to nearby Law Hospital after collapsing in the bathroom. She had suffered a stroke.

As I sped to the hospital, I vowed I would do everything I could to help and care for Margaret. From that moment on I was finished with ghosthunting.

My wife had no previous record of ill health but this was the beginning of a long battle with sickness that was to curse her for the rest of her life. In total she suffered two major strokes and five smaller strokes, known as 'continuations', which paralysed her. I became her full-time carer and did everything for her, along with assistance from Elizabeth and the nurses who would come to the house every day.

True to my word, I gave up the paranormal investigations. I was asked occasionally to comment on a story or suspected ghost by a newspaper or television programme but I never actively went out in the field. When Margaret died eight years after she was first struck down by the strokes, I continued to live a quiet life.

Slowly, however, thoughts of what I had devoted so much of my life to slipped back into my head. Thoughts of ghosts and thoughts of poltergeists. Thoughts of Lochmaben. The last one stronger than the rest.

I don't know why but that ghastly, grotesque figure I had stumbled across years earlier in the woods at Lochmaben wouldn't leave me. It haunted my thoughts daily. Perhaps it was because Margaret had come with me and she fell ill just afterwards. Maybe I was building a connection between the two events in my mind and making it personal. Whatever it was, I made the decision to go back to Lochmaben Castle and track down this creature.

I didn't know quite what I planned to do if I did come across it. Perhaps I would realise when the moment arrived. That may sound like a risky strategy but I had this burning passion inside of me that meant I had to return. I was scared to some extent but not apprehensive. Sometimes one allows the heart to rule the head and here I was, driving towards the unknown, alone and defenceless, at sixty-five years old.

I had made my way to Lochmaben in the early evening, much like my last visit years earlier. Of course, this time I was alone and I had decided to camp out in the woods, near the loch, rather than spend the night in the car.

As I set up my tent, the rain began to pour from the sky and soaked the dark-coloured clothes I hoped would camou-flage me. It was relentless through the night. I watched as the heavy rain lashed down on the loch and felt the night breeze blow into the tent. My mind was alert and ready for a sight less natural than this everyday scene I sat before at that moment. Much less natural.

It was nearing dawn when the rain finally ceased. I had stayed awake and sat by the tent all night, but had seen nothing. I went into the woods and made my way along a path by the lochside. If the creature wouldn't come to me, I would go looking for it.

I had walked some distance from the castle, which was no longer visible. By now I could see the main road through the trees and hear the sporadic sound of passing traffic.

I noticed a shadow beyond some shrubbery. I stopped and glared at the spot. It was the vampire. It walked slowly and purposefully and was stooped over like a hunchback. This was in contrast to my last encounter when it had me spinning as I attempted to follow its movements. I was shocked to see it

Through the trees and bushes of the wood surrounding Lochmaben
Castle, the hooded vampire was spotted by Tom upon his return to the
area after a long, self-imposed absence brought about by the illness
and eventual death of his wife, Margaret.

so close to the roadside, even if it was still dark under the trees.

It wore the same baggy attire from years before and old-fashioned criss-cross style boots on its feet. I slipped the camera I had carried with me from my pocket, put the viewfinder to my eye and pressed down on the button. I had a picture.

It stopped and turned its head towards me. The noise from the camera had alerted it to my presence. Now it was time to see how it would react. It glared at me with an evil intensity for what felt like a lifetime but in reality was probably just a few seconds. This grotesque beast looked like it had just crawled out of the grave. The greyness of its skin, blue protruding veins all over its face . . . it was horrendous. I summoned up all my courage and pointed the camera at it again before it suddenly scuttled off into the distance, this time on land, with a speed that looked unbecoming of it just moments earlier.

My heart pounded almost as quickly as the vampire drifted past trees.

Vampires, I thought, bloody vampires.

Despite encountering it twice now, I was still struggling to believe what I'd seen as I took slow steps backwards, peering through the tree branches and bushes for another sight of the monstrous creature. My left foot trod on something soft. I looked down and saw a small, lifeless rabbit. I crouched down beside it and examined the limp and deflated animal. Interestingly, there was no sign of blood. Usually, if it was a fox or another animal that had been behind the attack the prey would be ripped apart, its insides exposed and bloody. Not in this instance.

I stood up, gave a cursory glance for the creature, and returned my gaze to the ground as I followed the trodden-down path through the long grass. I quickly spotted another rabbit off to the side of the route, then another, and another. All

Just one of several rabbits discarded by the vampire and discovered by Tom amongst the trees near the banks of Castle Loch.

identical in death. I walked back and forth a few times and counted eight in total.

It was hard to comprehend but maybe this vampire had been feeding off the wildlife in the woods after all, just as the locals had suggested. With the speed it was capable of, it would have no problem snatching a rabbit, hare or any other creature that it fixed its soulless eyes upon. What I didn't understand was why it didn't venture out beyond the castle grounds under cover of darkness to feast on human flesh.

I made my way back to my tent, disassembled it in haste and scooped up all of my belongings. My actions weren't completely borne out of fear; I simply had no idea how to tackle this creature. My natural reaction had been to dismiss vampires as fiction but my mind was now changed. There's nothing like seeing a real-life Nosferatu in the flesh to make you question what you think you know in life. I have seen a lot of crazy stuff but nothing had prepared me for this encounter. This creature looked nothing like Christopher Lee and I certainly was no Peter Cushing. An exorcism would do nothing for a monster and I doubted crosses, holy water or a stake through the heart would make much difference either.

I reached my car and after digging in my pocket for the keys, I unlocked the boot and threw inside the items clutched under my left arm. I drove off as the morning sun broke through the clouds in the sky and this time there was no looking back in my rear-view mirror. I stared dead ahead until I reached the main road.

Weeks passed before I mentioned what I had seen to anyone. How would I start? The photographs were processed and, thank God, the creature was visible. I had taken two shots of the vampire but unfortunately its face wasn't visible in either. However, there was a clear side shot of it, hooded and head down. I went back to the photos again and again, reliving my encounter with it as if there were a movie playing in my head.

One afternoon I received a visit from an old friend. Davy was a keen greyhound man and would often drop by my house when he was in the area to get some tips for the next race meeting at Shawfield in Glasgow. He was also an experienced journalist who had written many stories about my investigations over the years and as we sat talking I confided in him. He could have caught flies in his mouth by the time I'd finished the story and his jaw nearly came loose when I passed him the photos.

Sensing a scoop he became excited and exclaimed the story had to be printed. I was a little reticent because I knew what I would have said had I read this story; the person concerned must be mad.

Davy was relentless though and, eventually, I submitted. I knew some people would laugh at me or say I was losing my marbles, but I had been there before decades earlier when I first went public with my paranormal investigations, so such a reaction would be nothing new.

My friend passed the details on to the features desk at the *Scottish Sun* and within days my extraordinary story and pictures were spread over two pages.

That's when the tale really took a turn into Weirdsville. It may be a well-worn cliché but I know better than anyone . . . life really is stranger than fiction.

Several months had passed since the *Sun* article when I received a letter in the post that really threw me. The American stamp in the corner and the New Orleans postmark had me intrigued. I wasn't to be let down.

I unfolded the sheet of paper and began to read the typed letter:

Mr Robertson, my name is Mary Grant. I represent a large group of people who at this moment in time would prefer to remain anonymous. I will contact you at a later date with full details. I am sure you shall understand when you read on. Regarding your article in the *Sun* newspaper in August 2001. (You are an amazing gentleman.) Would it be possible to catch it alive, or to get some skin or hair from it? Would it be possible for me to have one or two persons of our team sent over to accompany you. If you decide it can be successful. (Mr Robertson, money shall not be a problem.) Next time I contact you, I hope you have good news for us.

Mary Grant.

There was a PS, which read:

We have spent some time with Dolly the sheep. You come to us highly recommended. Mr Robertson if you can pull this of, you will be the most famous man on the planet.

I sat down in my armchair and placed the letter and its envelope on the table before me. I didn't know whether to laugh or be angry. My initial reaction was to treat it as a joke, especially since there were several spelling and grammatical errors and it generally didn't look too professional. Furthermore, there was no return address, which seemed strange if she wanted me to respond to the bizarre proposition.

I picked the envelope up and looked again at the date and location from where it was posted. New Orleans, Louisiana, 26 June 2002. That was quite some distance for a hoax to travel.

Although possible, it seemed unlikely that someone in the Deep South had read the Scottish version of the *Sun*. It wasn't even available online at that time. I also failed to understand why someone would wait nine months to send a hoax letter.

Maybe there was more to it. I read it again and shook my head in disbelief. What a letter. I picked it apart and tried to understand who this woman was and what she wanted. She needed it captured alive or for me at least to take some samples, I understood that. She had mentioned working with Dolly the Sheep. Dolly, of course, was the world's first cloned mammal, a remarkable and controversial experiment carried out by a team at Roslin Institute in Edinburgh in 1996. She quickly became the most famous animal in the world and truly was a scientific breakthrough.

I made a jump and wondered if this woman, Mary Grant, wanted the Lochmaben vampire captured in order to clone it. It sounded to me that she might have been claiming to be part of a scientific group, as she had mentioned other colleagues more than once in the abrupt letter.

To say I was intrigued was an understatement, so I passed it to Davy, who did some searches on the Internet. However, it was all too vague and he failed to find a Mary Grant that fitted the limited profile we had.

Two months had passed when I received another letter from Ms Grant. This time it was postmarked Houston, Texas, a neighbouring state to Louisiana, and dated 22 August. It read:

Mr Robertson, I've just arrived back from visiting our laboratory in Amsterdam. I fully intended to be in contact with you while visiting there with the prospect of inviting you over to see for yourself how well organised our team is. As you are well aware of how strange our trade is, we didn't get to spend as much time on this project as we would have liked due to technical problems in our laboratory, which means we shall be called back in the near future.

If you would be kind enough to join me and my team of four, you would be most welcome. And, of course, with your vast experience in this category you would be worth your weight in gold, as one says. I'm pleased to mention that it would be all expenses paid up front.

Now, concerning your own findings, we are all excited and hope you can do it. But you should be well aware that you will be smothered by the media. We would prefer our PR department to handle it all but it is entirely up to yourself how you wish to handle it at your end.

Mary Grant.

If anything, the second letter left me even more confused and in search of answers. That's if it wasn't a hoax, of course, and I couldn't yet rule that out.

But how did Mary Grant expect me to respond to any questions she asked of me if she never provided her contact details? It made no sense, but then again nothing did in this whole episode.

It was interesting to note that she mentioned a laboratory and the international connection, but the actual work they were conducting was still very much up for debate. And she still expected me to catch a damn vampire as if it were as simple as hooking a fish with a garden worm. Besides, I had absolutely no intention of returning to Lochmaben again.

Next, came a handwritten postcard from Mexico. It stated that progress was being made in the Latin American country with their latest project and they hoped to be back in Amsterdam sooner than expected. She was excited and wrote that she was sure this was the break they had been working towards and looked forward to our meeting in Amsterdam.

In trying to track down this mystery organisation I loaned the letters to people with Internet access and contacts in the media who I hoped may help. Rather foolishly, I didn't make back-up copies before I gave them out.

In total, I received four letters plus the postcard over a four-month period. The final two came shortly after Mary's second letter, from a man claiming to be part of her team. Sadly, these later letters were never returned to me. However, the content was much the same as the rest, frustratingly vague and full of hopeful wonderment.

On a cold winter's night in November 2002, I woke with a start to the sound of a ringing telephone. I jumped out of my bed, cursing the caller as I stumbled my way through the darkness, rubbing my bleary eyes.

I reached the phone before it stopped ringing and picked up the receiver.

'Hello?' I spat out angrily.

'Mr Robertson?' The person on the other end spoke with an American accent. At first, I thought it was a woman.

'Yes?' I replied curtly, ready to censure this person for calling in the wee hours.

'Mr Robertson, this is your little friend. I really hope you can help me. You'll have received the letters from Mary. I need help, please.'

The voice was effeminate, almost child-like, but I realised it was a man talking. It was a voice familiar to me but in that moment, tired and abruptly disturbed from sleeping, I couldn't place it.

'Who is this?' I asked. 'And how did you get my number? It's the middle of the night.'

'It's your little friend, Mr Robertson.' The line went dead.

I didn't know if he had hung up or if we had genuinely been cut off. If the truth be told, had the conversation lasted a moment longer, I was about to hang up. I checked for a number but it had been withheld, so I walked back to my bedroom in a haze, no longer from tiredness but confusion and bewilderment.

I lay in bed and stared at the ceiling. I didn't know what to do. If this was part of an ongoing prank it was maybe time to call the police, but how would I begin to explain the background?

I tossed and turned, sleeping intermittently and having strange dreams that weren't as weird as real life.

It was a struggle rising in the morning. I felt sluggish and lethargic from the lack of sleep and it took me a while to get going. It was probably around noon by the time I drove to the local store for my newspaper.

The shopkeeper greeted me as I walked through the door and tried to engage me in conversation but his voice was deaf to me as my eyes fixed on the newspaper stand. On every title, from tabloid to broadsheet, was a picture of Michael Jackson dangling his baby – her head covered with a blanket – over the balcony of a hotel in Germany to a crowd of fans and press on the pavement below. The headlines expressed anger and outrage at his crass stupidity but, to me, the pictures were almost like an epiphany.

I knew I had recognised the voice on the phone the night before, and as I picked up a newspaper and handed over the exact change to the shopkeeper, I realised why the child-like tone had sounded so familiar. It belonged to one of the most famous and controversial people on the planet. Wacko Jacko.

I had pulled into the driveway of my house before I realised where I was. My head was spinning but I knew I was not mistaken. Michael Jackson had called me in the middle of the night. He had asked for my help and referred to Mary Grant, the woman who claimed to have worked with Dolly the Sheep and who wanted me to catch a vampire.

I always felt Michael Jackson had severe mental problems, what with the constant surgery that left him unrecognisable from his younger self, and the bizarre antics that gained him such notoriety he was forced to defend his lifestyle in a court room.

Had a team of crackpot scientists been hired by Jackson to help him find a cure for his surgically damaged body? Or maybe something even crazier, to give him the gift of eternal life?

Maybe the King of Pop, who once lived in a ranch called Neverland, wanted to become a real life Peter Pan and never grow old.

I later learned that while Jackson had not performed in Scotland very often – in fact, he played just one concert in the country at Glasgow Green in 1992, where the noise levels were so loud he was apparently told by the city council he wouldn't be welcomed back – he did have a strange obsession with this wee corner of the globe. Stories that he wanted to buy a castle or stately home in Scotland often appeared in the tabloid news-papers, especially in 1997 when he visited several properties with his pregnant second wife, Debbie Rowe. They used the upmarket Cameron House Hotel at Loch Lomond as their base and looked over Glenmayne House in Galashiels and Invertrossachs House near Callander, but ultimately purchased neither. Rumours persisted on and off for the next decade that he wanted to set up home in Scotland although it never hap-pened.

His Scottish obsession didn't end there though. He was said to have recorded an album of Robert Burns songs with his friend, the ex-husband of Liza Minnelli, David Gest, and even his favourite Indian cuisine chef, Raj Bajwe, was a Scot.

Might Jackson also have turned to Scotland for a much more bizarre and extraordinary purpose?

As I entered my house I stared again at the picture on the front of the newspaper. Jackson and his team must have thought that by taking a sample of the blood from the vampire, a creature that had lived for hundreds of years, they could transfer the regenerative cells to Michael to either heal his damaged skin or make an attempt at granting eternal life. It sounded crazy, but then one only had to look at his life to realise nothing was out of the question.

That was my theory, but it appeared I would never know for sure, as the phone call was the last contact I had with Michael Jackson, Mary Grant or any of her associates. Whether it was the bad press from the hotel balcony incident that made him adopt a low profile for a while or he simply moved onto his latest mad idea, I don't know.

As for the vampire? Well, I never went back to Lochmaben. The story was out in the public and foretold is forewarned. I had no idea how to kill a vampire and even if I did, trying to get close to the creature was an impossible task in itself.

If the bizarre events originating from Lochmaben taught me anything, it was to prove that, no matter how old I was or what I had seen in my life, it was still possible to be left shocked and stunned.

And visitors to Lochmaben Castle beware, as there remains a macabre and otherworldly presence slinking around in those woods, baying for blood.

Epilogue

Barely a week would go by when I didn't think of Michael and the vampire, but I was convinced I would be forever in the dark about what it all really meant. The late night phone call on that winter's night in 2002 had been the final chapter in the incredible story, or so I had thought.

But then a shocking development led to an epilogue of epic proportions: on 25 June 2009, Michael Jackson died in his Los Angeles home, just weeks before his fifty-first birthday. The singer, who was due to begin an eight-month residency billed as his farewell tour in London's O2 Arena the following month, was discovered unconscious in his bedroom the morning after a concert rehearsal. He had suffered cardiac arrest and could not be resuscitated by his personal physician, Conrad Murray, who would later be arrested after the Los Angeles County Coroner stated that Michael's death was homicide, brought on by a cocktail of drugs in his system. It emerged that Jackson had been addicted to painkillers and other prescription drugs for many years, taking huge amounts of powerful medication such as Propofol, an anaesthetic administered in hospitals before surgical procedures.

The outpouring of grief around the world was immense. Mourning had not been seen on this level since the death of

Princess Diana twelve years earlier, and in this multimedia age was probably the biggest show business passing in history, overshadowing even Elvis's death. An estimated one billion people worldwide watched his live television memorial show, underlining the fact.

Inevitably, in the aftermath, there was a swathe of so-called friends, insiders, staff and hangers-on, who had a story they wished to tell the world, via the media, about the King of Pop. I'm a great believer in Fate and amongst literally hundreds of articles and reports, one story jumped out at me and had my heart racing.

In an exclusive interview with the *Daily Mirror* on 7 July, Jackson's former chauffeur, Al Bowman, revealed an amazing story that joined the dots to a picture I could previously only have imagined. Under the headline, 'LEAVE ME A CLONE – JACKSON'S BIZARRE PLEA TO STRANGE SECT. HE WANTED IDENTICAL VERSION OF HIMSELF', was the probable answer to why I had been asked to provide a blood sample from a vampire.

Al recounted how he had driven Michael and his friend, spoon bender Uri Geller, to a Las Vegas conference on human cloning in 2002. It was organised by a strange religious cult called the Raelians, who in turn have a scientific branch called Clonaid, which claims to have the ability to clone humans.

In the article, Al said:

Jackson was very excited. He bounced out of that conference like a small child. He was smiling and on a high. I heard him and Uri talking in the back of the limo. He was talking about the prospect of being cloned. He grabbed Uri by both arms and told him, 'I really want to do it, Uri, and I don't care how much it costs.'

I always remember Jackson talking about the cloning of Dolly

the Sheep in Britain in 1996. He was totally fascinated by it,'
Al continued. 'Then when he heard about the Raelians he
became utterly convinced this weird religious group could clone
humans. It was really oddball stuff but it interested Michael ...
[he] said he wanted a mini version of himself cloned to carry
on his legacy. He was hoping that Michael Jackson could live
forever.'

So much of what this chauffeur said resonated with me: Dolly
the Sheep, weird scientists and, of course, the date of the conference – 2002, the year I received the letters and phone
call.

The Raelian movement was established by a French journalist called Claude Vorhilon in 1974, after he claimed to have
been contacted by an extraterrestrial that told him humans
were created in laboratories 25,000 years ago by the Elohim,
beings from another planet. It is believed there could be as
many as 55,000 Raelian followers worldwide, preparing for
the return of the Elohim. The Clonaid offshoot targeted the
rich Hollywood community and, in 2002, made headlines
around the world when it claimed to have cloned the first
human, a baby girl named Eve.

The *Daily Mirror* article states that, after the Las Vegas conference, Jackson spoke with Clonaid managing director and
Raelian bishop Dr Brigette Boisselier about cloning. Indeed,
the day after Al Bowman's revelations, Dr Boisselier responded
via Clonaid's official website. While she said they had a policy
of never revealing their client's identities, she did praise
Jackson.

Clonaid prides itself on never releasing the identity of the
numerous individuals who have been cloned in the past six
years. Even if that policy has been at the cost of my reputation,

it's important for us that the celebrities and other interested parties contacting us know they won't be betrayed.

Michael was a visionary who wasn't afraid to embrace new technologies. I'm glad his interest in cloning is being revealed now, since he was a pioneer in his views about it back in 2002 and his fans ought to know about it.

Al ended the *Daily Mirror* interview by saying: 'When I heard Clonaid had cloned the first human being, I couldn't help thinking there was a mini Michael Jackson running around somewhere. With Michael, anything is possible.'

My God, I thought, as I closed the paper, you don't know the half of it.